TEACH YOURSELF

ARABIC

by

A. T. AYYAD

RULES OF READING AND WRITING

Published by
TA-HA PUBLISHERS LTD.
1, Wynne Road
London SW9 0BD

Reprinted 1996

ISBN 0 907461 13 1

Published by:
Ta-Ha Publishers Ltd.
1 Wynne Road
LONDON SW9 0BD

British Library Cataloguing in Publication Data

Ayyad, A.T.
Teach yourself Arabic.
Part 1: Rules of reading and writing
1. Arabic language—Grammar
I. Title
492′.782421 PJ6111

ISBN 0 907461 13 1

Printed in Great Britain by
DELUXE PRINTERS
245a Acton Lane,
London NW10 7NR.

Al Fatiha (the opening Sura of the Qur'an)

« سُورَةُ الفَاتِحَــةِ »

بِسْـمِ اللّـهِ الرَّحْمَـنِ الرَّحِيـمِ (١)

الحَمْـدُ لِلَّهِ ربِّ العَالَمِيـنَ(٢) الرَّحْمَنِ الرَّحِيـم (٣) مَالِكِ يومِ الدِّينِ (٤) إِيَّاكَ نعْبُدُ
وَ إِيَّاكَ نَسْتَعِينُ (٥) إهْدِنَا الصَّـراط المُسْتَقِيـم (٦) صِـرَاطَ الذِّينَ أنعَمْتَ عَلَيْهِمْ غَيْـرِ
المَغْضُـوبِ عَلَيْهِـمْ وَلاَ الضَّالِيـنَ (٧)

In the name of Allah the Compassionate, the Merciful (i) Praise be to Allah, the Master of the Universes (2) The Compassionate, the Merciful (3) The King of the Day of Judgement (4) It is Thee whom we adore, and it is of Thee we beg assistance (5) Lead us in the right way (6) The way of those to whom Thou has been gracious, not of those against whom Thou art incensed, nor of those who have gone astray (7).

NOTE

1. Read and write from right to left.

2. The stroke on the vowel ā, ī, ū means the vowel is elongated, thus it sounds: aa, ii, uu.

3. The apostrophe at the end of the middle of the word means a glottal stop.

4. The letter (ع) no. 18 has no english equivalent, and is transliterated with this mark ‘ .

5. The dot under the letter means an emphatic letter.

TABLE OF CONTENTS

Readings (cont.)

INTRODUCTION

Several years ago I lived among a most hospitable people, the people of England. During this time I was nominated, through the Egyptian Embassy in London, to give some Arabic lessons for beginners at Harrow Technical College.

Searching for a book in English valid for this aim, I found several about Arabic grammar, all very high standard works and very profound, but suitable only for scholars and university graduates. For teaching the elementary rules of reading and writing to young learners, I found none.

To prepare myself for the task of teaching technical college students, I was encouraged to compile this book. It is meant for adult English speaking learners but would also be suitable for children in English primary schools, provided some audio-visual aids are introduced fitting to their mentality and age.

After I graduated in 1930, I was appointed as a teacher of the Arabic language at the Lycee Francaise in Cairo, where I stayed for 23 years teaching and heading the Arabic section. It was a golden opportunity, throughout this period, to teach Arabic to hundreds of students of different nationalities and different ages and mentalities.

Besides this experience, I consulted and read with great interest and care the following Egyptian, English and American books:

1. Teach Yourself Arabic — by Professor A. S. Tritton of London University
2. A New Arabic Grammar — by J. A. Haywood and H. M. Nahmad
3. Arabic for English-Speaking Students — by M. 'Abdul Rauf, Ph.D.
4. An Introduction to Modern Arabic — by Farahat J. Ziadah and Bailey Winder
5. Introduction to Arabic, B.B.C. (Radio course for beginners) — by T. I. Mitchell and Dr. Barbour of the Department of Linguistics, University of London
6. Colloquial Arabic — by de Lacy O'Leary, D.D.
7. Beginning Arabic — by Sami A. Hanna (Middle East Centre, University of Utah) and Naguib Greis (Middle East Studies Centre, Portland State College). Forward by Aziz S. 'Atiya.
8. Written Arabic: An Approach to the Basic Structures — by A. F. L. Beeston, Laudian Professor of Arabic in the University of Oxford.

These books were useful and fitting enough to inspire the compilation of this book. To their authors I convey my sincere thanks.

This book dispenses entirely with rules of grammar, unless they are useful and equate with a rule of reading and writing. As a matter of fact, people never care for the rules of grammar when they deal with each other in their daily common affairs. But grammar surely is very useful and essential for acquiring the treasures of knowledge preserved in books.

The great Muslim Arab thinker Ibn Khaldoun stated in his famous book "Prolegomena" that 'grammar and rhetoric are two sides of the philosophy of the language and we should not start teaching them to the child until he reaches a suitable age.'

However, all the grammar notes mentioned in this book are not intended as a subject of study, but are merely meant to acquaint the learner with the nature and general structure of the language.

A simplified study of Arabic grammar is hopefully expected to appear in "Basic Arabic — Part 2".

This text-book is a modified prototype of the basic method of teaching Arabic to Arab students since the beginning of learning. As an unprecedented work in English, I shall be glad to consider your criticism and suggestions, and to collaborate with any progressive achievement, addressed to me through the publisher.

A. T. Ayyad

حُرُوفُ الهِجَاءِ (مُبَسَّطَة)

The Alphabet (simplified)

N.B. — Look carefully at the position of the letters above or below the line.

— Watch the dots carefully: their number and position.

No.	English symbol	Name	Part-Shaped	Full Form
1	a, i, u	alif	أ	أ
2	b	bā'	بـ	ب
3	t	tā'	تـ	ت
4	th	thā'	ثـ	ث
5	j	jīm	جـ	ج
6	ḥ	ḥā'	حـ	ح
7	kh	khā'	خـ	خ
8	d	dāl	د	د
9	dh	dhāl	ذ	ذ
10	r	rā'	ر	ر
11	z	zāy	ز	ز
12	s	sīn	سـ	س
13	sh	shīn	شـ	ش

Note: The first letter (no. 1) called Alif or Hamza, has the sound of the glottal stop as: (a) in amber, or (i) in inn, or (u) in zulu.

No.	English symbol	Name	Part-Shaped	Full Form
14	ṣ	ṣād	صـ	ص
15	ḍ	ḍād	ضـ	ض
16	ṭ	ṭā’	ط	ط
17	ẓ	ẓā’	ظ	ظ
18	‘	‘ayn	عـ	ع
19	gh	ghayn	غـ	غ
20	f	fā’	فـ	ف
21	q	qāf	قـ	ق
22	k	kāf	ـكـ or كـ	ك
23	l	lām	لـ	ل
24	m	mīm	مـ	م
25	n	nūn	نـ	ن
26	h	hā’	ـهـ or هـ	ه
27	w	wāw	و	و
28	y	yā’	يـ	ي

Arabic Letters

with sounds not found in standard english

Letter	Trans.	Name	Sound
ا . أ . ء	a	alif or hamza	Glottal stop (see footnote p. 2)
ح خ	ḥ kh	ḥā’ khā’	(h) with the sound of clearing the throat (ch) as in scottish loch
ص ض	ṣ ḍ	ṣād ḍād	(s) as in sun, with more emphasis (d) as in double, with more emphasis

Letter	Tans.	Name	Sound
ط ظ	ṭ ẓ	ṭā' ẓā'	(t) as in cut, with more emphasis (th) as in thus, with more emphasis
ع غ ق	ʻ gh q	ʻayn ghayn qāf	strong gutteral sound produced by compressing the throat and expulsion of breath (r) as in french with more gargling sound (c) as in column with emphasis from the throat

The term "hamza" and "alif" as well, denotes the sound of the glottal stop. Hamza takes the shape (ء) and comes always on the top of the letters أ . ؤ . ئ .

The rules of hamza will be explained in due course.

The alif in the beginning of the speech denotes always the glottal stop, even without the hamza.

Exercise

1. Write the alphabet (full and part-shaped form) three times, with their english equivalents, saying their names aloud.
2. (a) how many dotted letters in the alphabet and what are they?
   (b) how many undotted letters in the alphabet and what are they?
3. Identify: ل م ق ف ع د ر ذ ز س
   ص ش و ي غ ا خ ث ح ت
4. Try to memorise the alphabet in its recognised form.

How do you write Arabic?

كَيْفَ تَكْتُبُ العَرَبِيَّة ؟

The Arabic script is cursive, unlike the English which has separate printed forms.

In printed and written Arabic, all the letters join both following and preceding letters (as they do the same in English handwriting), except six letters, namely:

ا . د ذ . ر ز . و

They only join preceding letters. Hence they have taken the name of "stubborn letters", because they do not cooperate with their companions, as all other letters do. They join only the preceding letters, and refuse to join their successors.

The Stubborn Letters

They join preceding letters, but never join their successors

No.	Arabic	English symbol
1	ا	a
2	د	d
3	ذ	dh
4	ر	r
5	ز	z
6	و	w

The process of connecting the letters needs different forms.

My predecessors who wrote on the subject of Arabic language, to whom and their works I convey a high appreciation, took great care over the Arabic script, by using the traditional varying letters: isolated, initials, medials and finals, nevertheless confused the learner.

To avoid this kind of difficulty, I have simplified these four forms into two forms only:

1. The Part-Shaped Form is used for the construction of the word with joined letters, exactly in the same way as English handwriting, with the exception of the six Stubborn Letters which join only their preceding letters, but *never* join their successors.

2. The Full Form is used:

   (a) at the end of the words, and

   (b) if ever we want to write independent letters.

The classical and traditional method of teaching Arabic calligraphy is very important and essential for scholars and calligraphers.

Arabic calligraphy is considered one of the universal and fine arts. It embodies the language of one of the world's great civilisations and religions. It was hallowed as the vehicle of God's revelation in the Qurā'n, whose numerous and different manuscripts are taken as masterpieces of art.

But for an English speaking learner and for every beginner as well, it would be more practical and pragmatic to begin with the basic and most simplified rules of Arabic reading and writing and even rules of grammar.

Thus the learner can achieve the capacity to write in the same way he practices his English handwriting by means of:

(a) using and joining all the part-shaped forms, except the six stubborn letters which although they join their preceding letters never join their successors;

(b) using the full form letters only for the finals.

By means of this method, Arabic script will be easier and equate more with English handwriting.

In conclusion: write the Arabic word exactly as you would write an English word, but bear in mind these three points:

1. Write from right to left.

2. Use the part-shaped letters, as you normally use the letters in your English handwriting, but remember the exception of the six stubborn letters which join with precedings and detach from the successors.

3. For the finals use always the full form letters.

Connecting Letters Practice

تَدْرِيب وَصْل الحُرُوف

All words in Arabic consist of one to five letters for particles, to six for verbs and to seven for nouns. Here are groups of 2, 3, 4, 5, 6 and 7 connected letters covering all the alphabet in its recognised order, beginning with أ and ending with ي.

Note: (a) These groups have no meaning, but follow the order of the alphabet in order to show the process of connecting the letters.

(b) All the finals as a rule take the full form shape.

(c) Watch the stubborn letters carefully and see how they join, and how they separate.

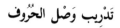

مَجْمُوعات وَصْل الحَـرُوف

A. Two Letters

أ. حَـرْفان

Connected Letters		Separated Letters	
ab	اب	a b	ا ب
tth	تث	t th	ت ث
jḥ	جح	j ḥ	ج ح
khd	خد	kh d	خ د
dhr	ذر	dh r	ذ ر
zs	زس	z s	ز س
shṣ	شص	sh ṣ	ش ص
ḍṭ	ضط	ḍ ṭ	ض ط
ẓʿ	ظـع = ظع	ẓ ʿ	ظ ع
ghf	غف	gh f	غ ف
qk	قك	q k	ق ك
lm	لم	l m	ل م
nh	نه	n h	ن ه
wy	وى	w y	و ى

B. Three Letters

ب. ثَـلاثَـة حُـرُوف

abt	ابت	a b t	ا ب ت
thjḥ	ثجح	th j ḥ	ث ج ح
khddh	خدذ	kh d dh	خ د ذ
rzs	رزس	r z s	ر ز س
shṣḍ	شصض	sh ṣ ḍ	ش ص ض
ṭẓʿ	ططـع = ططع	ṭ ẓ ʿ	ط ظ ع
ghfq	غفق	gh f q	غ ف ق
klm	كلم	k l m	ك ل م
nhw	نهو	n h w	ن ه و
y	ى	y	ى

C. Four Letters

ج. أرْبَعَـة حُـرُوف

Connected Letters			Separated Letters	
abtth	ابتث		a b t th	ا ب ت ث
jḥkhd	جحخد		j ḥ kh d	ج ح خ د
dhrzs	ذرزس		dh r z s	ذ ر ز س
shṣḍṭ	شصضط		sh ṣ ḍ ṭ	ش ص ض ط
ẓ‘ghf	ظعغف		ẓ ‘ gh f	ظ ع غ ف
qklm	قكلم	q k l m	q k l m	ق ك ل م
nhwy	نهوى		n h w y	ن ه و ى

D. Five Letters

د. خَمْسَـة حُـرُوف

abtthj	ابتثج	a b t th j	ا ب ت ث ج
ḥkhddhr	حخدذر	ḥ kh d dh r	ح خ د ذ ر
zsshṣḍ	زسشصض	z s sh ṣ ḍ	ز س ش ص ض
ṭẓ‘ghf	طظعغف	ṭ ẓ ‘ gh f	ط ظ ع غ ف
qklmn	قكلمن	q k l m n	ق ك ل م ن
hwy	هوى	h w y	ه و ى

E. Six Letters

هـ. سِـتة حُـرُوف

abtthjḥ	ابتثجح	a b t th j ḥ	ا ب ت ث ج ح
khddhrẓs	خدذرزس	kh d dh r ẓ s	خ د ذ ر ز س
shṣḍṭẓ ‘	شصضطظع	sh ṣ ḍ ṭ ẓ ‘	ش ص ض ط ظ ع
ghfqklm	غفقكلم	gh f q k l m	غ ف ق ك ل م
nhwy	نهوى	n h w y	ن ه و ى

F. Seven Letters

و. سَبْعَة حُرُوف

Connected Letters		Separated Letters	
abtthjḥkh	ابتثجحخ	a b t th j ḥ kh	ا ب ت ث ج ح خ
ddhrzsshṣ	دذرزسشص	d dh r z s sh ṣ	د ذ ر ز س ش ص
ḍṭẓ‘ghfq	ضطظعغفق	ḍ ṭ ẓ ‘ gh f q	ض ط ظ ع غ ف ق
klmnhwy	كلمنهوى	k l m n h w y	ك ل م ن ه و ى

Practice

Connected	Separated	Connected	Separated
نظر	ن ظ ر	كتب	ك ت ب
قعد = قعد	ق ع د	أكل	أ ك ل
نفع = نفع	ن ف ع	جلس	ج ل س
رقد	ر ق د	نزل	ن ز ل
نام = نام	ن ا م	خرج	خ ر ج
صام = صام	ص ا م	دخل	د خ ل
فتح = فتح	ف ت ح	قرأ	ق ر أ

Exercise

Answer: 1. What are the "Stubborn Letters"?

2. Why do we call them "Stubborn Letters"?

3. Write the following words in connected letters:

شرب	ش ر ب	أخذ	أ خ ذ
لعب	ل ع ب	فرح	ف ر ح
حسن	ح س ن	حمل	ح م ل
ضحك	ض ح ك	سرق	س ر ق
كسب	ك س ب	ضرب	ض ر ب
صعد	ص ع د	سمع	س م ع
قبل	ق ب ل	لبس	ل ب س
طبخ	ط ب خ	سعد	س ع د
فتح	ف ت ح	رضع	ر ض ع
فهم فهم	ف ه م	ركب	ر ك ب

How to read Arabic

كَيْفَ تَقْرَأ العَرَبِيّة

Basic Vowels

الحَرَكَاتُ الأساسِيّة

All the letters in Arabic are consonants. The consonants cannot achieve a full sound without vowels.

The letter "B" in English, for example, achieves different sounds by the aid of different vowels, e.g. ba - bi - bu - b (unvowelled).

The B in this example gives four different sounds, nevertheless it is one letter. The sounds occur with vowels a, i, u. Also it occurs by the absence of the vowel as the sound in the stop sounds B of the word ri<u>b</u>.

The Arabic alphabet is different. It consists of 28 consonants and has no written vowels to achieve the same sounds which occur in English letters. Thus, the vowels in Arabic are represented by signs written above or below the consonant. These signs are called in Arabic, harakat — حركات or vowel signs.

The basic vowel signs are four short vowels, from which nine other vowels are derived (4 + 9 = 13).

This means that every letter in the Arabic alphabet could be pronounced or read with 13 different sounds, although it is one and the same letter in all cases. Also, this means that the alphabet with its 28 consonants multiplies up to 28 × 13 = 364 different sounds, a huge number which might appear to be a terrible number.

This is a paradoxical difficulty because, as a matter of fact, all Arabic speakers hardly use these vowels at the end of the words in their daily conversation, or use their signs in their correspondance.

Books, printings and other mass media never use these vowel signs except on very rare occasions. They are used only in teaching beginners, and in important religious and literary texts. They are very useful and indispensible for scholars and grammarians who deal with classical Arabic.

The vowels signs are particularly essential in the preliminary stages of teaching English-speaking beginners. They are the foundation of the writing and reading rules. When learners get used to the rhythm of the language, they can dispense with the vowel signs.

The spoken living language is influenced by normal speech and by differences of dialect rather than the rules of grammar.

Moreover, the linguistic authorities of the past have left clear advice for the Arabic speaking world; the advice is to avoid all the final vowel signs. They say in their invaluable advice: ((سكّنْ تَسلَمْ)) — sakkin taslam — which means literally translated "Unvowel (the endings), deliver yourself of the error)".

In this context I might quote the following: "Willmore in his Spoken Arabic of Egypt (p. 10) makes this sensible remark, 'Take care of the consonants and the vowels will take care of themselves' ". *

So, let us hopefully try to explain the vowel signs:

The basic vowel signs are four, namely:

1. Fatḥa فَتْحَة

2. Kasra كَسْرَة

3. Ḍamma ضَمَّة

4. Sukūn سُكُون

*Colloquial Arabic (4th Edition, p. 14) by Dr. Lacy O'Leary.

Briefly, for example:

1. Fatḥa — فَتْحَة — is a stroke above the letter to replace the 'a' as in ba = بَ

2. Kasra — كَسْرَة — is a stroke below the letter to replace 'i' as in bi = بِ

3. Ḍamma — ضَمَّة — is a small و above the letter to replace 'u' as in bu = بُ

4. Sukun — سُكُون — is a circle above the letter to indicate the absence of the vowel (stop consonant) as in 'b' in rib (stop consonant) = بْ

1. Fatḥa فَتْحَة — ١

(Do not forget to read Arabic from right to left)

This is a stroke above the letter as in — tha = ثَ , ta = تَ , ba = بَ . It has the value of 'a' as in 'candid' or 'u' as in 'nut'. For example:

Meaning	Transliteration	Arabic Verb
to write or he wrote	kataba	كَتَبَ
to plant he planted	zara‹a	زَرَعَ
to study he studied	darasa	دَرَسَ

Note: Arab grammarians consider the verb as the heart of the sentence. It denotes the action and its time. The simplest form of the verb is the third person singular of the perfect tense. It is the root from which all derived forms, whether verbal or nominal, come. So the verb kataba, كَتَبَ — means 'to write' and 'he wrote' as well. The subject 'he' is hidden and unspoken but understood (For further explanation see p. 22).

Meaning		Transliteration	Arabic Verb
to eat	he ate	akala	أَكَلَ
to sit	he sat	jalasa	جَلَسَ
to descend	he descended	nazala	نَزَلَ
to stand	he stood	waqafa	وَقَفَ
to go out	he went out	kharaja	خَرَجَ
to enter	he entered	dakhala	دَخَلَ
to read	he read	qara'a	قَرَأَ
to explain	he explained	sharaḥa	شَرَحَ
to praise	he praised	madaḥa	مَدَحَ
to look	he looked	naẓara	نَظَرَ
to serve	he served	khadama	خَدَمَ
to escape	he escaped	haraba	هَرَبَ
to thank	he thanked	shakara	شَكَرَ
to destroy	he destroyed	hadama	هَدَمَ
to peel	he peeled	qashara	قَشَرَ
to wash	he washed	ghasala	غَسَلَ
to be present / to come		ḥadara	حَضَرَ
to tell the truth / he told . . .		ṣadaqa	صَدَقَ
to be good, right, proper		ṣalaha	صَلَحَ
to frown / to glower		‘ abasa	عَبَسَ
to cut	he cut	qaṭa‘a	قَطَعَ = قَطَعَ
to prevent	he prevented	mana‘a	مَنَعَ = مَنَعَ
to take off / to put off		khla‘a	خَلَعَ = خَلَعَ
to put	he put	wada‘a	وَضَعَ = وَضَعَ
to connect, combine, arive at		waṣala	وَصَلَ
to steal	he stole	saraqa	سَرَقَ

Fatḥa Practice

Read the following verbs:

to throw or	he threw	qadhafa	قَذَفَ
to separate	he separated	faṣala	فَصَلَ
to brag	he bragged	fashara	فَشَرَ
to weave	he weaved	nasaja	نَسَجَ = نَسَجَ
to wipe	he wiped	masaḥa	مَسَحَ = مَسَحَ
to guard	he guarded	harasa	حَرَسَ
to gather / to add		jamaʿa	جَمَعَ = جَمَعَ
to deceive	he deceived	khadaʿa	خَدَعَ
to forgive	he forgave	ghafara	غَفَرَ
to remember / to mention		dhakara	ذَكَرَ
to carry	he carried	ḥamala	حَمَلَ
to grant	he granted	wahaba	وَهَبَ
to describe	he described	waṣafa	وَصَفَ
to put	he put	waḍaʿa	وَضَعَ = وَضَعَ
to be head of		ra'sa	رَأَسَ
to rule / to judge		ḥakama	حَكَمَ
to be at / to strike		ḍaraba	ضَرَبَ
to knead	he kneaded	ʿajan	عَجَنَ = عَجَنَ
to cook	he cooked	ṭabakha	طَبَخَ = طَبَخَ
to appear	he appeared	ẓahara	ظَهَرَ = ظَهَرَ

Exercise تَمْرِين

Read aloud and re-write the following twice:

(he) wrote	كَتَبَ
(he) studied	دَرَسَ
(he) wrote and (he) studied	كَتَبَ وَ دَرَسَ
(he) ate	أَكَلَ
(he) thanked	شَكَرَ
(he) ate and (he) thanked	أَكَلَ وَ شَكَرَ
(he) read	قَرَأَ
(he) explained	شَرَحَ
*(he) read and (he) explained	قَرَأَ وَ شَرَحَ
(he) came in	دَخَلَ
(he) went out	خَرَجَ
*(he) came in then (he) went out	دَخَلَ فَخَرَجَ
(he) ploughed	حَرَثَ
(he) planted	زَرَعَ
(he) ploughed and then (he) planted	حَرَثَ فَزَرَعَ

*Note: wa وَ and fa فَ are to particles of conjunction. The waw و indicates mere combination without order; the fā' فَ implies combination with order. The second comes after the first. (For further explanation see p. 102).

2. Kasra ٢ – كَسْرَة

This is a stroke below the letter as in — thi = ثِ , ti = تِ , bi = بِ . It has the value of ‘i’ as in sit. For example:

to ride or	he rode	rakiba	رَكِبَ
to keep / preserve		ḥafiẓa	حَفِظَ
to lose	he lost	khasira	خَسِرَ
to be hidden,	he was hidden	khafiya	خَفِيَ
to win	he won	rabiḥa	رَبِـحَ = رَبِحَ
to play	he played	la‘iba	لَـعِبَ = لَعِبَ
to be sad	he was sad	hazina	حَزِنَ
to be joyful	he was joyful	fariḥa	فَرِحَ
to laugh	he laughed	ḍaḥika	ضَحِـكَ = ضَحِكَ
to hear	he heard	sami‘a	سَمِـعَ = سَمِعَ
to work / make		‘amila	عَمِلَ
to be content / pleased with		raḍiya	رَضِيَ
to ascend	he ascended	ṣa‘ida	صَـعِدَ = صَعِدَ
to praise / thank		ḥamida	حَمِدَ
to be ill	he was ill	mariḍa	مَرِضَ
to wear	he wore	labisa	لَبِسَ
to forget	he forgot	nasiya	نَسِيَ
to be happy	he was happy	sa‘ida	سَعِدَ = سَعِدَ
to drink	he drank	shariba	شَرِبَ
to be safe	he was safe	salima	سَلِمَ = سَلِمَ
to be thirsty	he was thirsty	‘aṭisha	عَطِشَ
to arrive	he arrived	qadima	قَدِمَ = قَدِمَ

to be angry	he was angry	ghaḍiba	غَضِبَ
to be dry	he was dry	yabisa	يَبِسَ
to accompany	he accompanied	saḥiba	صَحِبَ = صَحِبَ
to think / count		ḥasiba	حَسِبَ
to permit	he permitted	adhina	أَذِنَ
to accept	he accepted	qabila	قَبِلَ
to get tired / to toil		ta‘iba	تَعِبَ = تَعِبَ
to jeer / scoff / sneer		sakhira	سَخِرَ = سَخِرَ
to understand / comprehend		fahima	فَهِمَ = فَهِمَ
to wonder	he wondered	‘ajiba	عَجِبَ
to desire / wish / want		raghiba	رَغِبَ
to have sore eyes / to be inflamed (eyes)		ramida	رَمِدَ

Exercise

تَمْرِين

Read aloud and re-write the following three times:

to hear	سَمِعَ
to wonder	عَجِبَ
(he) heard and (he) wondered	سَمِعَ وَ عَجِبَ
to laugh	ضَحِكَ
to be happy	سَعِدَ
(he) laughed and (he) was happy	ضَحِكَ وَ سَعِدَ

to descend	نَزَلَ
to ascend	صَعَدَ
(he) descended and (he) ascended	نَزَلَ وَ صَعَدَ
to gain	رَبِحَ
to lose	خَسِرَ
(he) gained and (he) lost	رَبِحَ وَ خَسِرَ
to get thirsty	عَطَشَ
to drink	شَرِبَ
(he) got thirsty and (he) drank	عَطِشَ وَ شَرِبَ
to rejoice	فَرِحَ
to be sad	حَزِنَ
(he) rejoiced then (he) was sad	فَرِحَ فَحَزِنَ
to learn by heart	حَفِظَ
to forget	نَسِيَ
(he) learned by heart and then (he) forgot	حَفِظَ فَنَسِيَ
to eat	أَكَلَ
to be satisfied	شَبِعَ
(he) ate and (he) was satisfied	أَكَلَ وَ شَبِعَ
to play	لَعِبَ
to be safe	سَلِمَ
(he) played and (he) was safe	لَعِبَ وَ سَلِمَ

Grammar Note: This pattern of verb, if intransitive, usually denotes — joy and sadness, satiety and dissatisfaction, beauty and deformity or colour, such as:

to be joyful	فَرِحَ	to have a perfect figure	غَيِدَ
to be sad	حَزِنَ	to be with a rheumy eye	عَمِشَ
to be satisfied	شَبِعَ	to be green	خَضِرَ
to be thirsty	عَطِشَ		

3. Ḍamma

٣ – ضَمَّــة

This is a small و above the letter as in — thu = ثُ , tu = تُ , bu = بُ .
It has the value of 'u' as in Zulu. For example:

to be great or to become	ʿ azuma	عَظُمَ
to be small	ṣaghura	صَغُرَ
to be abundant	kathura	كَثُرَ
to be heavy	thaqula	ثَقُلَ
to be nice	ḥasuna	حَسُنَ
to be easy	sahula	سَهُلَ
to be difficult	ṣaʿuba	صَعُبَ
to be sweet	ʿadhuba	عَذُبَ
to be ugly	qabuḥa	قَبُحَ

This pattern of verb, if intransitive, indicates characteristics or features, eg:

to be witty	ظَرُفَ	to be nice	حَسُنَ
to be ugly	قَبُحَ	to be noble	شَرُفَ

Grammar Note:

Active and Passive — all the verbs which you have learned are called divested verbs, because every verb has three indispensible radical letters. These are the majority of verbs in Arabic and from which all other derivations, verbal or nominal, are formulated.

You can easily notice the first and the third letters are always vowelled with a fatha (ـَ), while the second is vowelled with a fatḥa, karsa or ḍamma, e.g.:

(a) fatḥa (ـَ) as in فَتَحَ = to open

or (b) kasra (ـِ) as in فَهِمَ = to understand

or (c) ḍamma (ـُ) as in سَهُلَ = to become easy

Also, all these verbs are in the simplest form of the verb, i.e. the third person singular of the perfect tense and they are all in the active mood. To formulate the passive mood of such verbs:

(a) change the fatḥa (ـَ) above the first letter to ḍamma (ـُ) and,

(b) change the vowel of the second letter to kasra (ـِ), e.g.:

Active		Passive	
he wrote	كَتَبَ	was written	كُتِبَ
he praised	مَدَحَ	was praised	مُدِحَ
he thanked	شَكَرَ	was thanked	شُكِرَ

Meaning	Transliteration	Passive	Active
was heard	sumiʿa	سُمِعَ	سَمِعَ
was played	luʿiba	لُعِبَ	لَعِبَ
was described	wuṣifa	وُصِفَ	وَصَفَ
was born	wulida	وُلِدَ	وَلَدَ
was wiped	musiḥa	مُسِحَ	مَسَحَ
"kept preserved"	ḥufiẓa	حُفِظَ	حَفِظَ
was ruled	ḥukima	حُكِمَ	حَكَمَ
was guarded	ḥurisa	حُرِسَ	حَرَسَ
was mentioned	dhukira	ذُكِرَ	ذَكَرَ
was washed	ghusila	غُسِلَ	غَسَلَ
was written	kutiba	كُتِبَ	كَتَبَ
was planted	zuriʿa	زُرِعَ	زَرَعَ
was studied	durisa	دَرَسَ	دُرِسَ
was eaten	ukila	أُكِلَ	أَكَلَ
was explained	shuriḥa	شُرِحَ	شَرَحَ
was praised	mudiḥa	مُدِحَ	مَدَحَ

Exercise

تَمْرِين

Change the following verbs into passive tense and write their meanings:

Meaning	Passive	Active
was put	وُضِعَ	وَضَعَ
was ridden	رُكِبَ	رَكِبَ
was hit	ضُرِبَ	ضَرَبَ

Meaning	Passive	Active
was peeled	قُشِر	قَشَرَ
was cooked	طُبِخ	طَبَخَ
was stolen	سُرِق	سَرَقَ
was understood	فُهِم	فَهِمَ
was emptied	فُتِح	فَتَحَ
was worn	لُبِس	لَبِسَ
was forgotten	نُسِي	نَسِيَ

4. Sukūn

٤ - سُكُون

This is a small circle above the letter as in — Smit<u>h</u> = ثْ , bi<u>t</u> = تْ , and ri<u>b</u> = بْ

It is a sign of unvowelled letters or stop consonants. Sukūn in Arabic means quiescence, eg. no sound uttered after pronouncing the consonant, indicating the absence of the vowel, for example:

Meaning	Transliteration		Arabic word
how?	kaifa	Interrogatives	كَيْفَ ؟
where?	ayna		أَيْنَ ؟
how many?	kam		كَمْ ؟
who?	man as (sun)		مَنْ ؟

Meaning	Transliteration		Arabic Word
I	ana	Pronouns	أَنا
we (m.f.)	naḥnu		نَحْنُ
you (m.s.)	anta		أَنْتَ
you (f.s.)	anti		أَنْتِ
you (m.pl.)	antum		أَنْتُمْ
he	huwa		هُوَ
she	hiya		هِيَ
they (m.pl.)	hum		هُمْ
from	min	Prepositions	مِنْ
away from	ʻan		عَنْ

Sukūn Practice

Meaning	Transliteration	Arabic Word
who* (are) you? (m.)	man anta	مَنْ أَنْتَ ؟
who (are) you? (f.)	man anti	مَنْ أَنْتِ ؟
who (is) he?	man huwa	مَنْ هُوَ ؟
who (is) she?	man hiya	مَنْ هِيَ ؟
who (are) they? (m.pl)	man hum	مَنْ هُمْ ؟
who (are) you? (m.pl)	man antum	مَنْ أَنْتُمْ ؟

*Notice the absence of the verb to be in Arabic (for more pronouns see p. 103, and prepositions p. 103).

Meaning	Transliteration	Arabic Word
how (are) you (m.s.)	kaifa anta	كَيْفَ أَنْتَ ؟
how (are) you? (f.s.)	kaifa anti	كَيْفَ أَنْتِ ؟
how (is) he?	kaifa huwa	كَيْفَ هُوَ ؟
how (is) she?	kaifa hiya	كَيْفَ هِيَ ؟
how (are) you? (m.pl.)	kaifa antum	كَيْفَ أَنْتُمْ ؟
where (is) 'Omar?*	anya 'omar	أَيْنَ عُمَرْ؟
where (is) Hind?	anya hind	أَيْنَ هِنْدُ ؟
how many (are) you? (m.pl)	kam antum	كَم انْتُمْ ؟
how many (are) they? (m.pl)	kam hum	كَمْ هُمْ ؟
I and you	ana wa anta	أَنَا وأَنْتَ
he and she	huwa wa hiya	هُوَ وَهِيَ
he (is) 'Omar	huwa 'omar	هُوَ عُمَرْ
she (is) Hind	hiya hind	هِيَ هِنْدُ
you (are) a boy	anta walad	اَنْتَ وَلَدُ
she (is) a girl	hiya bint	هِيَ بِنْتُ
we and you (m.pl.)	naḥnu wa antum	نَحْنُ وَ انْتُمْ
he kepy away from 'Omar	ba uda an 'omar	بَعُدَ عَنْ عُمَرَ
he (is) from London	huwa min London	هُوَ مِنْ لَنْدَن
he (is) from Egypt	huwa min Misr	هُوَ مِنْ مِصْر
I and you and he and she	ana wa anta wa huwa wa hiya	انَا وَ أنْتَ وَهُوَ وَهِيَ
'Omar and Hind	'omar wa hind	عُمَرْ وَ هِنْدُ

*Notice the absence of capital letters in Arabic as عُمَر . You can benefit by the advice of the authorities (Sakkin Taslam, p. 13). As a rule, unvowel the ending letters whenever and wherever you pause.

Exercise تَمْرِين

Translate into English:

English	Arabic
I am a boy	اَنَا وَلَدٌ
He is Omar	هُوَ عُمَرُ
She is a girl	هِيَ بِنْتٌ
You are from London	انْتَ مِنْ لَنْدَن
You are from Egypt	انْتَ مِنْ مِصْرَ
How are you?	كَيْفَ انْتَ ؟
I am Omar and you are Hind	اَنَا عُمَرُ وَ أنْتِ هِنْدُ
Who are you?	مَنْ أنْتُمْ ؟

Translate into Arabic:

English	Arabic
You (are) ‘Omar	أنْتَ عُمَرُ
How (are) you?	كَيْفَ هالَكَ
She (is) Hind	هِيَ هِنْد
How (is) she?	كيف هالك
He kept away from ‘Omar	بعد عن عُمَر
How many are they?	كم هم

Prolongation

"al Madd" (آلْمَـدّ)

The following vowel signs are short vowels:

(a) Fatḥa فَتْحَة as Ba = بَ

(b) Kasra كَسْرَة as Bi = بِ

(c) Ḍamma ضَمَّة as Bu = بُ

1. The fatḥa (ـَ) changes from a short vowel to an elongated vowel if it is followed by an alif أ, eg:

   *tā (taa) تَا , bā (baa) بَا , ā (aa) آ .

2. Also, the kasra (ـِ) changes from a short vowel to an elongated vowel, if it is followed by yā' ى , eg:

   tī (tii) تِي , bī (bii) بِي , ī (ii) اِي .

3. Also, the ḍamma changes from a short vowel to an elongated vowel, if it is followed by waw و , eg:

   **tū (tuu) تُو , bū (buu) بُو , ū (uu) اُو .

*Notice: the alif ا is put on top of the initial hamza and takes this shape آ , instead of اا . When the alif ا follows ل lam alif ال they are written thus لا .

**The alif ا , the yā' ي, and the waw و in this case become vowel signs and are called long vowels.

The Long Fatḥa

اَلِف اَلْمَد

Meaning	Transliteration	Word
door	bāb	بَاب
fang, tusk	nāb	نَاب
youth	shāb	شَاب
he said	qāla	قَالَ
slept	nāma	نَامَ
stood up	qāma	قَامَ
fasted	ṣāma	صَامَ
to flow, become liquid	sāla	سَالَ

The Long Kasra

يَاءُ اَلْمَد

Meaning	Transliteration	Word
generous	karīm	كَرِيم
subtle	latīf	لَطِيف
dear	‘azīz	عَزِيز
big	kabīr	كَبِير
small	ṣaghīr	صَغِير
long	ṭawīl	طَوِيل
short	qaṣīr	قَصِير

The Long Damma

وَاوُ اَلمَـد

Meaning	Transliteration	Word
bugle	būq	بُوق
(very) patient	ṣabūr	صَبُور
forgiving	ghafūr	غَفُور
very thankful	shakūr	شَكُور
devoted, fond	wadūd	وَدُود
stick, cane, reed	ūd	عُود
spiteful	ḥaqūd	حَقُود
frowning, gloomy	‘ abūs	عَبُوس
pole, post	‘ amūd	عَمُود
cluster, bunch of grapes	‘ unqūd	عُنْقُود
envious	ḥasūd	حَسُود
submissive, humble	khanū ‘	خَنُوع
written	maktūb	مَكْتُوب
planted	mazrū ‘	مَزْرُوع
described	mawsūf	مَوْصُوف
studied	madrūs	مَدْرُوس
eaten	ma’kūl	مَأْكُول
washed	maghsūl	مَغْسُول
reaped, harvested	maḥsūd	مَحْصُود

Practice

تَـدريب

Meaning	Transliteration	Word
market	sūq	سُوق
camel caravan	‘ ir	عِير
fig	tīn	تِين
beloved	ḥabīb	حَبِيب
loaf	raghīf	رَغِيف
harem	ḥarīm	حَرِيم
end	ākhir	آخِر
Adam	Ādam	آدَم
Children of Adam (human race)	banū Ādam	بَنُو آدَم
hearts	qulūb	قُلُوب
lions	usūd	أُسُود
professor	ustādh	أُسْتَاذ
Prince	amīr	اَمِير
vizier	wazīr	وَزِير
sultan	sulṭān	سُلْطَان
iron	ḥadid	حَدِيد
new	jadīd	جَدِيد
cheap	rakhīs	رَخِيص
Ramadan (month of fasting)	ramaḍān	رَمَضَان

Table of Basic Vowels

مَمْدُودَةٌ Elongated	قَصِيرَةٌ Short	اَلْحَرَكَةُ Vowel
kātib كَاتِب is writing/writer	kataba كَتَبَ he wrote	fatḥa فَتْحَةٌ
salīm سَلِيم sane, safe	salima سَلِمَ to be safe	kasra كَسْرَةٌ
waqūr وَقُور grave, solemn	waqura وَقُرَ to be solemn	ḍamma ضَمَّةٌ
(there is no long sukun)	yaktub يَكْتُبُ he writes	sukun سُكُونٌ

The Arabic numerals are as follows:

٥ Khamsa 5	٤ Arba' a 4	٣ Thalātha 3	٢ Ithnīn 2	١ Wahid 1
١٠ 'ashara 10	٩ Tis 'a 9	٨ Thamania 8	٧ Saba' a 7	٦ Sitta 6

Exercise تَمْرِين

Give three words for each of the following vowels and write in English the meaning of each word:

Vowel		Word		Meaning
Short Fatḥa فَتحَة"	١ ٢ ٣	مَدَحَ فَشَرَ خَدَعَ	1 2 3	to praise to brag to deceive
Short Kasra كَسْرَة"	١ ٢ ٣	حَفِظَ خَسِرَ عَجِبَ	1 2 3	to keep to lose (a game) to wonder
Short Ḍamma ضَمَّة"	١ ٢ ٣	وُصِفَ حُرِسَ شُرِحَ	1 2 3	was described was guarded was explained
Sukūn سُكُون"	١ ٢ ٣	كَمْ؟ مَنْ؟ مِنْ	1 2 3	How many? Who? from
Elongated Fatḥa اَلِف اَلْمَدّ	١ ٢ ٣	قَام صَام سَال	1 2 3	stood up fasted flowed
Elongated Kasra يَاءُ اَلْمَدّ	١ ٢ ٣	عَزِيز لَطِيف صَغِير	1 2 3	dear kind, subtle small
Elongated Ḍamma وَاوُ اَلْمَدّ	١ ٢ ٣	عَمُود حَسُود خَنُوع	1 2 3	post / pole envious humble

The Derived Vowels

اَلْحَرَكاتُ اَلْفَرْعِيَّة

The derived vowels are three types:

1. Nunation (تَنوين Tanwīn)
2. Doubling (تَشْدِيد Tashdid)
3. Nunation and doubling both together
   (تَنْوِين وَتَشْدِيد Tanwīn and Tashdid)

Each type has three forms:

one with fatḥa فَتْحَة
one with kasra كَسْرَة
one with ḍamma ضَمَّة

1. Nunation

(Tanwīn تَنْوِين)

Nunation has the value of the indefinite article 'a' or 'an' in English. Also it indicates singularity. It occurs only at the end of nouns and adjectives when indefinite.

(a) Two fatḥas ١ – فَتْحَتَان

(Accusative case ending)

The double fatḥa above the final letter gives the sound of 'ann' أن , pronounced but unwritten, with an ا added to the final. This is called nunation تَنْوِين e.g.

الخ	ثً = ثاً	تً = تاً	بً = باً
* etc.	than = tha	tan = ta	ban = ba

Meaning and Case	Transliteration	Word
a door (accusative)	bāban	بَاباً
a girl (accusative)	bintan	بِنْتاً
a boy (accusative)	waladan	وَلَداً

(b) Two Kasras ب – كَسْرَتَان

(Genetice case ending)

The two kasras below the final letters give the sound of 'inn' إنْ
It is pronounced but not written, e.g.

الخ	ثٍ = ثِ	تٍ = تِ	بٍ = بِ
etc.	thin = thi	tin = ti	bin = bi

Meaning and Case	Transliteration	Word
a door (genetive)	babin	بَابٍ
a girl (genetive)	bintin	بِنْتٍ
a boy (genetive)	waladin	وَلَدٍ

* الخ is an abbreviation for إلى آخِرِه , ila akhirih (lit. to its end) which means etc. or and so forth. (Other abbreviations come in due course.) (see pp. 98–99).

(c) Two Ḍammas ضَمَّتَانِ – ج

(Nominative case ending)

The two dammas above the final letter, give the sound of 'un' اُنْ , pronounced but not written, e.g.

الخ	ثٌ = ثُ	تٌ = تُ	بٌ = بُ
etc.	thun = thu	tun = tu	bun = bu

Meaning	Transliteration	Word
a door (nominative)	bābun	بَابٌ
a girl (nominative)	bintum	بِنْتٌ
a boy (nominative)	waladun	وَلَدٌ

Note: The (ا) is added only to the final letter in the accusative case.

Practice

Case	Meaning	Transliteration	Word
Nom.	a man	rajulun	رَجُلٌ
Nom.	a river	nahrun	نَهْرٌ
Nom.	a dog	kalbun	كَلْبٌ
Nom.	a heart	qalbun	قَلْبٌ
Nom.	a pen	qalamun	قَلَمٌ
Nom.	a book	kitabun	كِتَابٌ

Case	Meaning	Transliteration	Word
Acc.	a man	rajulan	رَجُلاً
Acc.	a river	nahran	نَهْراً
Acc.	a dog	kalban	كَلْبًا
Acc.	a heart	qalban	قَلْبًا
Acc.	a pen	qalaman	قَلَماً
Acc.	a book	kitaban	كِتَابًا
Gen.	a man	rajulin	رَجُلٍ
Gen.	a river	nahrin	نَهْرٍ
Gen.	a dog	kalbin	كَلْبٍ
Gen.	a heart	qalbin	قَلْبٍ
Gen.	a pen	qalamin	قَلَمٍ
Gen.	a book	kitabin	كِتَابٍ

A and THE

اَلتَّنْوِين وَ أَدَاةُ التَّعْرِيف

As is known, nunation has the value of 'A' in English. It occurs at the end of nouns or adjectives only, represented by ـً with an (ا) in the accusative, ـٌ in the nominative and ـٍ in the genetive.

اَلْ — al, has the value of 'the' in English prefixed and attached to nouns or adjectives. The nouns, in such cases, lose their nunation, e.g.

Meaning & Case	Transliteration	Definite	Indefinite
the door* (nom.)	al bābu	اَلْبَابُ	بَابٌ
the girl (nom.)	al bintu	اَلْبِنْتُ	بِنْتٌ
the boy (nom.)	al waldu	اَلْوَلَدُ	وَلَدٌ
the door (acc.)	al bāba	اَلْبَابَ	بَاباً
the girl (acc.)	al binta	اَلْبِنْتَ	بِنْتاً
the boy (acc.)	al walada	اَلْوَلَدَ	وَلَداً
the door (gen.)	al bābi	اَلْبَابِ	بَابٍ
the girl (gen.)	al binti	اَلْبِنْتِ	بِنْتٍ
the boy (gen.)	al waldi	اَلْوالَدِ	وَلَدٍ

*The cases will be explained in due course.

Practice تَدْرِيب

Indefinite		Definite	
Meaning	Word	Meaning	Word
the king	al maliku اَلْمَلِكُ	a king	malikum مَلِكٌ
the house	al baytu اَلْبَيْتُ	a house	baytun بَيْتٌ
the land	al arḍu اَلأَرْضُ	a land	arḍun اَرْضٌ
the human-being	al insānu اَلانْسَانُ	a human-being	insānun إِنْسَانٌ
the servant	al khādimu اَلْخَادِمُ	a servant	khādimun خَادِمٌ
the father	al abu اَلأَبُ	a father	abun أَبٌ
the brother	al akhu اَلأَخُ	a brother	akhun أَخٌ
the sister	al ukhtu اَلأُخْتُ	a sister	ukhtun أُخْتٌ
the paper	al waraqu اَلْوَرَقُ	a paper	waraqun وَرَقٌ
the cup	al finjanu اَلْفِنجَانُ	a cup	finjanun فِنْجَانٌ
the sea	al baḥru اَلْبَحْرُ	a sea	baḥrun بَحْرٌ
the banana	al mawzu اَلْمَوْزُ	a banana	mawzun مَوْزٌ
the donkey	al ḥimāru اَلْحِمَارُ	a donkey	ḥimārun حِمَارٌ
the horse	al ḥiṣānu اَلْحِصَانُ	a horse	ḥiṣānun حِصَانٌ

2. Doubling

(Tashdid تَشْدِيد)

To double a letter in English you write it twice, whereas it remains one letter only in Arabic with the sign (ّ) above it. This sign is called shadda شَدَّة .

(a) Shadda with fatḥa أ – شَدَّة مع فَتْحَة

Meaning	Transliteration	Word
he smelled	shamma	شَمَّ *
he poured	ṣabba	صَبَّ
he counted	‘adda	عَدَّ

(b) Shadda with damma ب – شَدَّة مَعَ ضَمَّة

he smells	yashumma	يَشُمُّ
he pours	yaṣubbu	يَصُبُّ
he counts	ya‘uddu	يَعُدُّ

(c) Shadda with kasra ج – شَدَّة مَعَ كَسْرَة

he prays	yuṣallī	يُصَلِّي
to greet	yusallimu	يُسَلِّم
to kiss	yuqabbilu	يُقَبِّلُ

*The double letter مَّ consists of two associated letters. The first is unvowelled with sukun ْ and the second is vowelled with fatha َ thus: and so forth
شَمْمَ = شَمَّ

3. Nunation and Doubling both together

(Tanwīn and Tashdīd تَنْوِين وَتَشْدِيد معاً)

(a) Shadda with double fatḥas ا – شَدَّة مع فَتْحَتَيْن

Meaning and Case	Transliteration	Word
an uncle (acc.)	ʻ amman	عَمّاً
love, amity (acc.)	wuddan	وُدّاً
piety, devoutness (acc.)	birran	بِرّاً

(b) Shadda with double kasras ب – شَدَّة مع كَسْرَتَيْن

an uncle (gen.)	ʻammin	عَمٍّ
love, amity (gen.)	wuddin	وُدٍّ
piety, devoutness (gen.)	birrin	بِرٍّ

(c) Shadda with double ḍammas ج – شَدَّة مع ضَمَّتَيْن

an uncle (nom.)	ʻammun	عَمٌّ
love, amity (nom.)	wuddun	وُدٌّ
piety, devoutness (nom.)	birrun	بِرٌّ

Here we end with all basic and derived vowel signs in Arabic, explained and analysed.

Derived Vowels اَلْحَرَكات اَلْفَرعِيَّة

Practice تَدْرِيب

1. Tanwīn ١ – تَنْوِينٌ

Two ḍammas ضَمَّتَان (nominative)	Two kasras كَسْرَتَان (genetive)	Two fatḥas فَتْحَتَان (accusative)
سَمَكَةٌ	سَمَكَةٍ	a fish سَمَكَةً
طِفْلٌ	طِفْلٍ	a child طِفْلاً
صُنْدُوقٌ	صُنْدُوقٍ	a box صُنْدُوقاً
جَيْشٌ	جَيْشٍ	an army جَيْشاً
فَرَحٌ	فَرَحٍ	joy فَرَحاً
قَمَرٌ	قَمَرٍ	a moon قَمَراً
يَوْمٌ	يَوْمٍ	a day يَوْماً
اِسْمٌ	اِسْمٍ	a noun اِسْماً
جَرِيدَةٌ	جَرِيدَةٍ	a newspaper جَرِيدَةً

2. Tashdīd ٢ – تَشْدِيدٌ

With damma مَعَ ضَمَّة	With kasra مَعَ كَسْرَة	With fatha مَعَ فَتْحَة
he escapes يَفِرُّ	he teaches يُعَلِّمُ	he escaped فَرَّ
he passes by يَمُرُّ	he educates يُرَبِّي	he passed by مَرَّ
he aligns يَصُفُّ	he whistles يُصَفِّرُ	he aligned صَفَّ
he loves, wishes يَوَدُّ	he arranges يُرَتِّبُ	he loved, liked وَدَّ
he stretches يَمُدُّ	he glorifies يُمَجِّدُ	he stretched مَدَّ
he pulls يَشُدُّ	he extols يُسَبِّحُ	he pulled شَدَّ

3. Tanwin and Tashdid both together

٣ – شَـدَّة وَتَنْوين مَعًا

English	Transliteration	Arabic
'Omar is an Egyptian (nominative)	'Omar miṣriyyun	عُمَر مِصْريٌّ
Charles is an Englishman (nom.)	Charle engliziyyun	شَارْل اِنجليزيٌّ
Aristotle is a Greek man (nominative)	Aristo yunāniyyun	أَرِسْطو يونانيٌّ
de Gaulle is a Parisian (nominative)	Digōl parisiyyun	دِيجُول بَارِيسيٌّ

*A noun takes the nominative case when it is the doer of the verb or the subject or predicate of a nominal sentence, subject ((عُمَر)) predicate ((اِنْجليزيٌّ)) Words such as 'miṣriyyun' etc. formed in this way are adjectives and the (ى) is called 'yā annisba — يَاء النِسبَة and means 'pertaining to'.

He praised an Egyptian (acc.)	madaḥa miṣriyyan	مَدَحَ مِصْرِيًّا
He praised an Englishman (acc.)	madaḥa engliziyyan	مَدَحَ اِنْجليزيًا

A noun takes the accusative case when it is the object.

He came with an Englishman	harda m'a ingliziyyin	حَضَرَ مع اِنْجليزيٍّ
He came with an Egyptian	harda m'a miṣriyyin	حَضَرَ مَعَ مِصْريٍّ
He came with a Greek man	harda m 'a yunaniyyin	حَضَرَ مَعَ يُونَانيٍّ

A noun takes the genetive case when it occurs after a preposition.

Vowel Signs and their English Equivalent

اَلْحَرَكاتُ وَمَا يُقَابِلُها بالانجليزيَّة

	Basic Vowel Signs			Equivalents
	Short Vowels			
1	Fatḥa	بَ (الخ)	١	ba (etc.)
2	Kasra	بِ	٢	bi
3	Ḍamma	بُ	٣	bu
4	Sukun	بْ	٤	b
	Elongated Vowels			
	Fatḥa	بَا		bā (etc.)
	Kasra	بِي		bī
	Ḍamma	بُو		bū
	Derived Vowel Signs			
5	Two fatḥas (nunation)	باً	٥	ban (etc.)
6	Two kasras (nunation)	بٍ	٦	bin
7	Two ḍammas	بٌ	٧	bun
8	Shadda and fatḥa	بَّ	٨	bba (etc.)
9	Shadda and kasra	بِّ	٩	bbi
10	Shadda and ḍamma	بُّ	١٠	bbu
11	Shadda and 2 fatḥas	بّاً	١١	bban (etc.)
12	Shadda and 2 kasras	بٍّ	١٢	bbin
13	Shadda and 2 ḍammas	بٌّ	١٣	bbun

Table of All Vowel Signs

جَدْوَلُ اَلْحَرَكات جميعها

Derived فَرْعِيَّةٌ							Basic أساسِيَّةٌ		
Nun. & Dblng.		Doubling		Nunation		Elongated	Short	Sign	
تَنْوِينٌ وتَشْدِيدٌ		تَشْدِيدٌ		تَنْوِينٌ		مَمْدُودَة	قَصِيرَة	اَلْحَرَكة	
مِصْرِيّاً	١١	شَمَّ	٨	بَاباً	٥	نَامَ	وَزَنَ	فَتْحَةٌ	١ –
مَصْرِيٍّ	١٢	يُنَظِّفُ	٩	بَابٍ	٦	يَطِيرُ	شَرِبَ	كَسْرَةٌ	٢ –
مِصْرِيٌّ	١٣	يَشُمُّ	١٠	بَابٌ	٧	يَصُومُ	قَرُبَ	ضَمَّةٌ	٣ –
							مَنْ ؟	سُكُونٌ	٤ –

The numerals are as follows:

عَشَرَةٌ	تِسْعَةٌ	ثَمَانِيَةٌ	سَبْعَةٌ	سِتَّةٌ	خَمْسَةٌ	اَرْبَعَةٌ	ثَلاَثَةٌ	اِثْنَانِ	وَاحِدٌ
١٠	٩	٨	٧	٦	٥	٤	٣	٢	١
10	9	8	7	6	5	4	3	2	1

أحَدَ عَشَرَ اِثْنا ١٠ ثَلاثَة ١٠ اَرْبَعَةَ ١٠ خَمْسَةَ ١٠ سِتَّةَ ١٠ سَبْعَةَ ١٠ ثَمانِيَةَ ١٠ تِسْعَةَ ١٠ عُشْرُون

٢٠	١٩	١٨	١٧	١٦	١٥	١٤	١٣	١٢	١١
20	19	18	17	16	15	14	13	12	11

Combined figures take the English order, thus:

٥٤٨٠	٢٢٠٤	١٠١١	٥٠٥	٣٠٥	٢٠٤	١٠٢	١٠١	١٠٠
5480	2204	1011	505	305	204	102	101	100

How do you formulate the Active Participle?

(Three lettered verb)

(كَيْفَ تَصُوغُ اِسْمَ اَلْفَاعِلِ مِنَ الثُّلاثي)

The active participle of verbs of three integral radicals takes the measured form of: e.g. Doer = فَاعِلٌ

(for further explanation, see p. 110)

كَتَبَ = كَاتِبٌ   ضَرَبَ = ضَارِبٌ

It is a noun or adjective void of time sense as well as denoting the meaning of the present tense, thus expressing two meanings in one form, e.g.:

I (am) a writer (m.) *or* I am writing	ana katibun	اَنَا كَاتِبٌ	*
I (am) a writer (f.) *or* I am writing	ana katibatun	اَنَا كَاتِبَةٌ	**
You (are) a writer (m.) *or* you are writing	anta katibun	اَنْتَ كَاتِبٌ	
You (are) a writer (f.) *or* you are writing	anti katibatun	اَنْتِ كَاتِبَةٌ	
He (is) a writer *or* he is writing	huwa katibun	هُوَ كَاتِبٌ	
She (us) a writer *or* she is writing	hiya katibatun	هِيَ كَاتِبَةٌ	

*Notice the absence of the verb to be in Arabic

**This ة in كَاتِبَةٌ is a combination of ت and ه , it is called 'closed' - tā' تَاء مَرْبُوطَة
It is the most common feminine sign. When it is vowelled it sounds 't' تَ . If it has no vowel it sounds 'h' ه .

Practice

تَدْرِيب

Meaning		Active Participle	Verb
donor	is granting	وَاهِبٌ	وَهَبَ
robber	is robbing	سَارِقٌ	سَرَقَ
murderer	is murdering	قَاتِلٌ	قَتَلَ
guardian	is guarding	حَارِسٌ	حَرَسَ
carrier	is carrying	حَامِلٌ	حَمَلَ
ruler	is ruling	حَاكِمٌ	حَكَمَ
conqueror	is conquering	فَاتِحٌ	فَتَحَ
interpreter	is interpreting	شَارِحٌ	شَرَحَ
farmer	is farming	زَارِعٌ	زَرَعَ
labourer	is labouring	عَامِلٌ	عَمِلَ
receiver	is receiving	قَابِلٌ	قَبِلَ
listener	is listening	سَامِعٌ	سَمِعَ
seeker	is seeking	بَاحِثٌ	بَحَثَ
player	is playing	لَاعِبٌ	لَعِبَ

Exercise

تَمْرِينٌ

Give the active participle of the following verbs and write in the meaning of each:

Meaning	Active Participle	Verb
farmer	زَارِع	زَرَعَ
guard	حَارِس	حَرَسَ
carrier	حَامِل	حَمَلَ
listener	سَامِع	سَمِعَ
arriver	قَادِم	قَدِمَ
labourer	عَامِل	عَمِلَ
winner	رَابِح	رَبِحَ
friend / companion	صَاحِب	صَحِبَ
player	لَاعِب	لَعِبَ
thanker	شَاكِر	شَكَرَ
servant	خَادِم	خَدَمَ
drinker	شَارِب	شَرِبَ
frowner	عَابِس	عَبَسَ

How ~~to~~ do you formulate the Passive Participle?

(Three lettered verb)

(كَيْفَ تَصُوغُ اِسْمَ اَلْمَفْعُولِ مِنَ الثلاثي)

The passive participle of the verb of three integral radicals takes the measured form of: e.g. (to be) done مَفْعُولٌ

(to be) written كَتَبَ = مَكْتُوبٌ

It is a noun or adjective void of time sense as well as denoting the meaning of the past participle, thus expressing two meanings in one form.

Meaning	Passive Participle	Verb
(to be) beaten *or* the beaten (. . .)	مَضْرُوبٌ	ضَرَبَ
(to be) supported *or* the supported (. . .)	مَنْصُورٌ	نَصَرَ
(to be) planted *or* the planted (. . .)	مَزْرُوعٌ	زَرَعَ
(to be) opened *or* the opened (. . .)	مَفْتُوحٌ	فَتَحَ
(to be) eaten *or* the eaten (. . .)	مَأْكُولٌ	اَكَلَ
(to be) drunk *or* the drunk (. . .)	مَشْرُوبٌ	شَرِبَ

Meaning	Passive Participle	Verb
(to be) closed *or* the closed (. . .)	مَقْفُولٌ	قَفَلَ
(to be) seen *or* the seen (. . .)	مَنْظُورٌ	نَظَرَ
(to be) accepted *or* the accepted (. . .)	مَقْبُولٌ	قَبِلَ

Practice

English	Arabic
The door (is) opened	اَلْبَابُ مَفْتوحٌ *
the opened door	اَلْبابُ المَفْتوحُ
an opened door	بَابٌ مَفْتوحٌ
The book (is) new	اَلْكِتاب جدِيدٌ
the new book	اَلْكِتابُ اَلْجَدِيدُ
a new book	كِتَابٌ جَدِيدٌ
The guardian (is) honest	الحارِسُ امِينٌ
the honest guardian	الحارسُ الأَمينُ
an honest guardian	حارسٌ امِينٌ
The army (is) triumphant	الْجيشُ مَنْصورٌ
the triumphant (victorious) army	الجيشُ المَنْصورُ
a triumphant (victorious) army	جيشٌ مَنْصورٌ

*Such a sentence in Arabic is called a nominal sentence and is composed of subject and predicate. Note the absence of the verb to be. (See p. 60).

Exercise تَمْرِينٌ

Read aloud and re-write three times:

English	Arabic
1. Are you a teacher?	١ – هَل انْتَ مُدَرِّسٌ ؟
2. Yes, I am a teacher.	٢ – نَعَمْ ! انَا مُدَرِّسٌ
3. Is she a teacher?	٣ – هَلْ هيَ مُدَرِّسَةٌ ؟
4. Yes, she is a teacher.	٤ – نَعَمْ ! هيَ مُدَرِّسَةٌ
5. I am a doctor and he is a teacher.	٥ – انا طَبيبٌ وَهُوَ مُدَرِّسٌ .
6. 'Omar is an intelligent pupil.	٦ – عُمَرُ تِلْميذٌ ذَكيٌ
7. She is an intelligent girl.	٧ – هيَ بِنْتٌ ذَكِيَّةٌ
8. Who is he (this)?	٨ – مَنْ هَذَا ؟
9. This is Charles.	٩ – هَذا شَارل .
10. Charles is an Englishman.	١٠ – شَارْلُ اِنْجليزيٌ
11. The book is new.	١١ – اَلْكِتَابُ جَديدٌ
12. The river is long.	١٢ – اَلْنَهْرُ طَويلٌ

Note: هَلْ is a particle which introduces interrogative sentences; it has the equivalent meaning of 'est ce-que' in French.

Exercise تَمْرِينٌ

Translate into English: تَرْجِم إلى الانجليزيّة

English	Arabic
1.	١ أَنَا مِصْرِيٌّ وَأَنْتَ اِنْجليزِيٌّ
2.	٢ أَنْتَ تِلْمِيذٌ كَرِيمٌ
3.	٣ هَلْ أَنْتَ انْجليزِيٌّ ؟
4.	٤ هِيَ بِنْتٌ ذَكِيَّةٌ
5.	٥ هَذا قَلَمٌ
6.	٦ هَذَا كِتابٌ
7.	٧ أَنْتَ مُهَنْدِسٌ وَأَنا مُدَرِّسٌ
8.	٨ كَيْفَ أَنْتَ ؟
9.	٩ مَتَى خَرَجَ ؟
10.	١٠ أَيْنَ جَلَسَ ؟
11.	١١ هُوَ مِصْرِيٌّ وَهِيَ انْجليزِيَّةٌ
12.	١٢ أَنْتَ تِلْمِيذٌ عَاقِلٌ
13.	١٣ هِيَ بِنْتٌ عَاقِلَةٌ
14.	١٤ اَلْحَارِسُ أَمِينٌ

Again to "THE"
عَوْدٌ اِلى (اَلْ)

As is known, al اَلْ is the equivalent of 'the' in English, prefixed and attached to nouns and adjectives.

The alphabet consists of 28 consonants, which are divided into 2 categories:

A. Letters pronounced with the top of the tongue which are -

ت ث د ذ ر ز س ش ص

ض ط ظ ن ل

As the lam (ل) of اَلْ is pronounced with the top of the tongue, there is a phonetic incapacity to pronounce two letters at once with the top of the tongue. So, the lam (ل) is integrated in such letters in pronunciation, but still written, e.g.

(indefinite) sun = shamsun شَمْسٌ

(definite) the sun = ash-shamsu اَلْشَّمْسُ

Hence, these letters are called the 'sun letters'

اَلْحُرُوفُ اَلْشَّمْسِيَّة

B. The other 14 letters which are -

ا ب ج ح خ ع غ ف ق ك

م ه و ى

They are pronounced either from the throat or from the two lips and they are normally prefixed with اَلْ , e.g.

(indefinite) moon = qamarun قَمَرٌ

(definite) the moon = al-qamaru اَلْقَمَرُ

Hence, these letters are called the ‘moon letters’.

اَلْحُرُوف اَلْقَمَرِيَّةُ

‘Al’-the, could be written in both cases either without the hamza as ال , or with a sign called ‘wasala’ وَصْلَةٌ , a small ص over the alif, as ٱل .

Here are examples for all the ‘sun letters’: اَلْحُرُوفُ اَلشَّمْسِيَّةُ

Trans.	Definite Noun		Trans.	Indefinite Noun		
at-tilmīdhu	the pupil	اَلتِّلْمِيذُ	tilmīdhun	a pupil	تِلْمِيذٌ	١
ath-thawbu	the cloth	اَلثَّوْبُ	thawbun	a cloth	ثَوْبٌ	٢
ad-darsu	the lesson	اَلدَّرْسُ	darsun	a lesson	دَرْسٌ	٣
adh-dhaylu	the tail	اَلذَّيْلُ	dhaylun	a tail	ذَيْلٌ	٤
ar-rajulu	the man	اَلرَّجُلُ	rajulun	a man	رَجُلٌ	٥
az-zārafatu	the giraffe	اَلزَّرَافَةُ	zarafatun	a giraffe	زَرَافَةٌ	٦
as-samāu’	the sky	اَلسَّمَاءُ	samāu’n	sky	سَمَاءٌ	٧
ash-shamsu	the sun	اَلشَّمْسُ	shamsun	sun	شَمْسٌ	٨
aṣ-ṣayfu	the summer	اَلصَّيْفُ	ṣayfun	a summer	صَيْفٌ	٩
aḍ-ḍayfu	the guest	اَلضَّيْفُ	ḍayfun	a guest	ضَيْفٌ	١٠
at-tai’ratu	the airplane	اَلطَّائِرَةُ	tāi’ratun	an airplane	طَائِرَةٌ	١١
az-zifru	the finger-nail	اَلظِّفْرُ	ẓifrun	a finger-nail	ظِفْرٌ	١٢
an-niṣru	the eagle	اَلنِّسْرُ	niṣrun	an eagle	نِسْرٌ	١٣
al-laylu	the night	اَللَّيْلُ	laylun	a night	لَيْلٌ	١٤

The Moon Letters اَلْحُرُوفُ اَلْقَمَرِيَةُ

Trans.	Definite Noun	Trans.	Indefinite Noun
al-asadu	the lion الأَسَدُ	asadun	a lion أَسَدٌ ١
al-bābu	the door اَلْبَابُ	bābun	a door بَابٌ ٢
al-jamalu	the camel اَلْجَمَلُ	jamalun	a camel جَمَلٌ ٣
al-hmāru	the donkey اَلْحِمَارُ	hmārun	a donkey حِمَارٌ ٤
al-khabaru	the news اَلْخَبَرُ	khabarun	news خَبَرٌ ٥
al-aynu	the eye اَلْعَيْنُ	aynun	an eye عَيْنٌ ٦
al-ghurābu	the crow اَلْغُرابُ	ghurābun	a crow غُرَابٌ ٧
al-fa'ru	the mouse اَلفَأْرُ	fa'run	a mouse فَأْرٌ ٨
al-qamaru	the moon اَلْقَمَرُ	qamarun	a moon قَمَرٌ ٩
al-kitabu	the book اَلْكِتَابُ	kitābun	a book كِتَابٌ ١٠
al-maktabu	the bureau اَلْمَكْتَبُ	maktabun	a bureau مَكْتَبٌ ١١
al-haramu	the pyramid اَلْهَرَمُ	haramun	a pyramid هَرَمٌ ١٢
al-wardatu	the rose اَلْوَرْدَةُ	wardatun	a rose وَرْدَةٌ ١٣
al-yamamatu	the wild pigeon اَلْيَمَامَةُ	yama-matun	a wild pigeon يَمَامَةٌ ١٤

Note:

1. Nunation is the sign of indefiniteness and singularity.
2. (ال) is the sign of definiteness, so nunation disappears.
3. The sun letter is duplicated. The lam (ل) is written but not pronounced. It is integrated in the sun letter.

Practice تَدْرِيبٌ

Read aloud and re-write three times:

English	Arabic
1. The summer (is) hot.	١ الصَّيْفُ حَارٌّ
2. The sky (is) blue.	٢ السَّمَاءُ زَرْقَاءُ
3. The airplane (is) fast.	٣ الطَّائِرَةُ سَرِيعَةٌ
4. The night (is) dark.	٤ اللَّيْلُ مُظْلِمٌ
5. The sun (is) rising.	٥ الشَّمْسُ مُشْرِقَةٌ
6. The lesson (is) easy.	٦ الدَّرْسُ سَهْلٌ
7. The book (is) useful.	٧ الكِتَابُ نَافِعٌ
8. The dress (is) clean.	٨ الثَّوْبُ نَظِيفٌ
9. The door (is) opened.	٩ اَلْبَابُ مَفْتُوحٌ
10. The camel (is) patient.	١٠ اَلْجَمَلُ صَبُورٌ
11. The giraffe (is) an animal.	١١ الزَّرَافَةُ حَيَوانٌ
12. The pigeon (is) a bird.	١٢ اَلْحَمَامَةُ طَائِرٌ

Sentence Structure

تَكْوِيـنُ الجُملَةِ

There are two basic types of sentences: (a) the verbal sentence, and

(b) the nominal sentence

1. The Verbal Sentence

١ اَلْجُمْلَةُ اَلْفِعْلِيَّـةُ

The verbal sentence is one that is introduced by a verb, active or passive, and composed of the verb and its subject (doer), e.g.

'Omar wrote	كَتَبَ عُمَرُ
(subject/verb)	(فِعْلٌ فَاعِلٌ)

or, the substitute of the doer, which comes only with the passive, e.g.

The lesson was written	كُتِبَ الدَّرْسُ
*(substitute/passive verb)	(فِعْلٌ نَائِبُ فَاعِلٍ)

Note: The verb always precedes its subject-doer and its substitute. When the doer or the substitute of the doer is the subject of the verb, both assume *the nominative case.*

*To formulate the passive, see p. 22

Practice تَدْرِيبٌ

Meaning	Sentence	Subject	Verb
'Omar laughed	ضَحِكَ عُمَرُ	عُمَرُ	ضَحِكَ
The boy gained	رَبِحَ اَلْوَلَدُ	اَلْوَلَدُ	رَبِحَ
The camel became thirsty	عَطِشَ اَلْجَمَلُ	اَلْجَمَلُ	عَطِشَ
The pupil succeeded	نَجَحَ التِّلْمِيذُ	التِّلْمِيذُ	نَجَحَ
The player played	لَعِبَ اللَّاعِبُ	اللاعِبُ	لَعِبَ
the man went out	خَرَجَ الرَّجُلُ	الرَّجُلُ	خَرَجَ
The guest entered	دَخَلَ الضَّيْفُ	الضَّيْفُ	دَخَلَ
The lion roared	زَأَرَ الأَسَدُ	اَلأَسَدُ	زَأَرَ
The moon appeared	ظَهَرَ اَلْقَمَرُ	اَلْقَمَرُ	ظَهَرَ
The dress was cleaned	نَظُفَ اَلثَّوْبُ	اَلثَّوْبُ	نَظُفَ
The loaf was eaten	أُكِلَ الرَّغِيفُ	الرَّغِيفُ	أُكِلَ
The lesson was explained	شُرِحَ الدَّرْسُ	الدَّرْسُ	شُرِحَ
The dog was beaten	ضُرِبَ اَلْكَلْبُ	اَلْكَلْبُ	ضُرِبَ
The lesson was understood	فُهِمَ الدَّرْسُ	الدَّرْسُ	فُهِمَ

Exercise تَمْرِينٌ

Find out the missing word, and compose a verbal sentence and translate it into English.

Translation	Sentence	Subject or Substitute	Verb
			دَخَلَ
			خَرَجَ
			نَزَلَ
			ظَهَرَ
			فَهِمَ
			كَتَبَ
			حَفِظَ
			ضُرِبَ
			أُكِلَ
			لُبِسَ
			مُدِحَ
			سَهُلَ
			فُتِحَ
			طَارَ

Sentence Structure (cont.)

تَكْوِينُ ٱلْجُمْلَةِ (تابع)

2. The Nominal Sentence

٢ ٱلْجُمْلَةُ الاِسْمِيَّةُ

The nominal sentence is one that is introduced by a noun or a pronoun, and is composed of the subject, (ٱلْمُبْتَدَأ), and the predicate (ٱلْخَبَرُ)
The predicate may be:

(a) a noun or adjective, e.g.

(noun) 'Omar is a pupil — عُمَرُ تِلْمِيذٌ

(adj.) He (is) intelligent — هُوَ ذَكِيٌّ

(b) verbal or pronominal, e.g.

(verbal) 'Omar wrote the lesson — عُمَرُ كَتَبَ الدَّرْس

(pron.) 'Omar, his lesson is easy *or* 'Omar's lesson (is) easy — عُمَرُ دَرْسُهُ سَهْلٌ

(c) a quasi-sentence, prepositional or adverbial phrase, e.g.

(prep.) Victory (is) for us — اَلنَّصْرُ لَنَا

(adv.) The pupil (is) in front of the teacher — التِّلْمِيذُ امامَ ٱلْمُدَرِّسِ

Note: The absence of the verb to be (is). Also there is no equivalent to the verb 'to have'. Both the subject and the predicate of a nominal sentence assume *the nominative case.*

Practice تَـدْرِيب

Meaning	Nominal Sentence	Predicate	Subject
I (am) a teacher	أَنَا مُدَرِّسٌ	مُدَرسٌ	أَنَا
‘Omar (is) a pupil	عُمَرُ تِلمِيذٌ	تِلْمِيذٌ	عُمَرُ
The sky (is) blue	السَّمَاءُ زَرْقَاءُ	زَرْقَاءُ	اَلْسَّمَاءُ
The book (is) opened	اَلْكِتَابُ مَفْتُوح	مَفْتوحٌ	اَلْكِتَابُ
‘Omar understood the lesson	عُمَرُ فَهِمَ الدَّرْسَ	فَهِمَ الدَّرْس	عُمَرْ
He (is) in the garden	هُوَ في اَلْحَديقَةِ	في اَلْحَدِيقَةِ	هُوَ
You (are) on top of the house	اَنْتَ فَوْق اَلْبَيْتِ	فَوْقَ اَلبَيْتِ	اَنْتَ
She (is) beautiful	هيَ جَمِيلَةٌ	جَمِيلَةٌ	هيَ
The girl (is) beautiful and intelligent	اَلبِنْتُ جَمِيْلَةٌ وَذَكِيَّةٌ	جَمِيْلَةٌ وَذَكِيَّةٌ	اَلْبِنْتُ
The night (is) long	اَلَّيْلُ طَوِيلٌ	طَوِيلٌ	اَللَّيْلُ
The player (is) in the playground	اللاَّعِبُ في اَلْمَلْعَبِ	في اَلْمَلْعَبِ	اللاَّعِب
The day-time is short	النَّهَارُ قَصِيرٌ	قَصِيرٌ	اَلْنَّهَارُ

Exercise تَمْرِينٌ

Read and sort out the subject and predicate of the following:

1. The lion is the king of the animals	١ – اَلأَسَدُ مَلِكُ اَلْحَيَوَانِ
2. The loaf is fresh	٢ – اَلرَّغِيفُ طَازَجٌ
3. The mouse is a small animal	٣ – اَلْفَأْرُ حَيَوَانٌ صَغِيرٌ
4. The pyramid is a wonder	٤ – اَلْهَرَمُ أُعْجُوبَةٌ
5. The great pyramid is one of the world's wonders	٥ – اَلْهَرَمُ الأَكْبَرُ أَحَدُ عَجَائِبِ الدُّنْيَا
6. The rose is red	٦ – اَلْوَرْدَةُ حَمْرَاءُ
7. The eagle is the king of the birds	٧ – النِّسْرُ مَلِكُ الطُّيُور
8. The airplane flies in the sky	٨ – الطَّائِرَةُ تَطِيرُ فِي السَّمَاءِ
9. The sun is shining	٩ – الشَّمْسُ سَاطِعَةٌ
10. The sun-rise is a beautiful sight	١٠ – شُرُوقُ الشَّمْسِ مَنْظَرٌ جَمِيلٌ
11. Peace be upon you!	١١ – السَّلامُ عَلَيْكُم !
12. Allah is greater (exclamation, exaltation)	١٢ – اَللّٰهُ أَكْبَرُ !
13. Allah is ever living!	١٣ – اَللّٰهُ حَيٌّ !
14. (and) Upon you be peace! (in answer to 'peace be upon you')	١٤ – وَعَلَيْكُم السَّلام !

Rules of Hamza

قَوَاعِدُ اَلْهَمْزَةِ

To finish the basic rules of reading and writing, we must say a word concerning the rules of 'hamza'.

The hamza (ء)* denotes the sound of a glottal stop. The Arabic glottal stop may occur at the beginning, in the middle, or at the end of the word, unlike the English glottal stop which only takes place at the beginning of the word, represented by the vowels a, e, i, o or u.

The Initial Hamza

The hamza (ء) is placed on the alif (ا) if it occurs at the beginning of the word and no matter what its vowels may be, thus:

(he) took	(akhadha)	أَخَذَ
was taken	(ukhidha)	أُخِذَ
if (conditional article)	(in)	أَنْ = إِنْ

The Final Hamza

The final hamza (ـء) is written according to the preceding vowel:

(a) if the preceding vowel is ـَ place the hamza on a (أ)

(b) if the preceding vowel is ـِ place the hamza on a (ئ)

(c) if the preceding vowel is ـُ place the hamza on a (ؤ)

*See foot-notes, ps. 2 & 4.

(d) if the preceding vowel is ْ or a long vowel, place the hamza on the line independeltly – for example:

(a)	he read	(qara'a)	قَرَأَ	
(b)	was read	(quria')	قُرِئَ	
(c)	became pretty	(wḍna')	وَضُؤَ	
(d)	load	('ib'un)	عِبْءٌ	(sukun)
	sky	(samā'un)	سَمَاءٌ	(long vowel)
	slowly	(batī'un)	بَطِيءٌ	(long vowel)
	ablution	(wuḍū'un)	وُضُوءٌ	(long vowel)

The Middle Hamza

The hamza in the middle of the word has several rules, all of which are rather complicated for a beginner. However, there is a rule* which can be applied to the great majority of words and which is based on a phonetic adaptation, as follows:

(a) lift the stress on the glottal stop (ء) uttering it without any stress

(b) catch the uttered sound and distinguish then to what letter (ا) (و) or (ى) it relates and so place the hamza on the letter thus distinguished, e.g.

*If I remember correctly, I read in the "Arrisala «الرِّسَالَة» " – a well-known literary magazine issued in Cairo more than 30 years ago, that this rule is ascribed to Professor A. S. Tritton of London University.

he asked	(sa'ala)	سَأَلَ
he was asked	(su'ila)	سُئِلَ
a question	(su'alun)	سُؤَالٌ
banquet	(ma'dubatun)	مَأْدَبَةٌ
a well	(bi'run)	بِئْرٌ

If the hamza (ء) comes with ـَـ after a long vowel ا or و , place it on the line independently, e.g.

to draw a good omen	(tafa'ala)	تَفَاءَلَ
humanity (the ideal of mankind)	(muru'atun)	مُرُوءَةٌ

Examples أَمْثِـلَةٌ

Beginning		Middle		End	
to permit	أَذِنَ	to show mercy	رَأَفَ	to create	بَرَأَ
permission	إِذْنٌ	to show mercy	رَؤُفَ	to be free	بَرِئَ
then	إِذَنْ	merciful	رَؤُوفٌ	to be slow	بَطُؤَ
an ear	أُذُنٌ	revenge	ثَأْرٌ	innocents (p)	أَبْرِيَاءُ
a father	أَبٌ	to yawn	تَثَاءَبَ	innocent (s)	بَرِيءٌ
a mother	أُمٌّ	purity	وَضَاءَةٌ	harbours	مَوَانِئُ
a sister	أُخْتٌ	to be miserable	بَئِسَ	flat/level land	بَطْحَاءُ
furnace	أَتُونٌ	roar	زَئِيرٌ	slowness	بُطْءٌ
trace/track	أَثَرٌ	weary/bored	سَئِمَ	start/beginning	بَدْءٌ
camels	إِبِلٌ	weary/fed up	سَؤُومٌ	principle	مَبْدَأٌ
was eaten	أُكِلَ	fault/sin	خَطِيئَةٌ	start/beginning	ابْتِدَاءٌ

Readings - مُطَالعَاتٌ

Let us pause here and once again recall the rules of reading and writing and observe their application in the following readings.

To facilitate reading you can benefit from the invaluable advice of the authorities, i.e. unvowel all the endings and read Arabic in the way in which you read English.

Naturally, the indeclinables will keep their ending signs. This allowance will not spoil the meaning or the style.

All the nunated and vowelled endings will be unvowelled and have (سُكُونٌ–ْ) . It is a general rule to unvowel the ending letters whenever or wherever you pause.

In spoken Arabic, declension is never regarded. Only in the study of classical Arabic is it *essential and indispensible.* For common usage, you can manage without it.

The following are examples of modern spoken Arabic in a style known by the intelligentsia. Some stories are similar to those which the people use in the daily life.

١ بَيْنَ عُمَرَ وَشَارْل

1. A conversation between ‘Omar and Charles

‘Omar is an Egyptian youth*	عُمَرُ شَابٌ مِصْرِيٌّ
(and) he is a polite and intelligent student;	وَهُوَ طَالِبٌ مُؤَدَّبٌ وَذَكِيٌّ
(and) Charles is an English youth	وَشَارْل شَابٌ انجليزيٌّ
(and) he is a polite and intelligent student.	وَهُوَ طَالِبٌ مُؤَدَّبٌ وَذَكِيٌّ
‘Omar came from his country	حَضَرَ عُمَرُ مِنْ بَلَدِهِ
Egypt to London	مِصْرَ الى لَنْدَن ،
to study car engineering.	لِيَدْرُسَ هَنْدَسَةَ اَلْسَّيَّاراتِ
(And) Charles was also	وَكَانَ شَارْل أَيْضاً
studying car engineering	يَدْرُسُ هَنْدَسَةَ اَلْسَّيَّاراتِ
at the Faculty of Technology.	فِي كُلِّيَّةِ اَلْتِّكْنُولُوجِيا
Both (the two) were acquainted	تَعَارَفَ الاثْنَانِ
(and) friendship began to increase	وَأَخَذَتِ اَلْصَّدَاقَةُ تَزْدَادُ
between them day after day.	بَيْنَهُمَا يَوْماً بَعْدَ يَوْمٍ

*Unlike the English, the noun precedes the adjective in Arabic. The adjective agrees with the qualified noun in - cases of declension, gender, number and definiteness or indefiniteness (see further, p. 112).

(And in a day) One day,	وَفي يَوْمٍ
Charles said to ‘Omar –	قَالَ شَارْل لِعُمَرَ :
“I have heard and read	سَمِعتُ وَقَرأْتُ
much about Egypt	كَثِيراً عَنْ مِصْرَ ،
and (about) its ancient monuments	وَعَنْ آثَارِهَا اَلْقَدِيمَةِ
such as the Pyramids and the Sphinx	كَالْهَرَمِ و (أَبو اَلْهَوْلِ)
and the magnificent mosques.	وَالْمَسَاجِدِ اَلْعَظِيمَةِ
And (I am in need of) I want to visit it.	وَعَاوِز أَزُورُهَا ،
So, will you supply me	فَهَلْ تزَوِّدُني
with some useful instructions	بِبَعْضِ مَعْلُومَاتٍ نافِعَةٍ
(in) for my conversations with the people?”	في حَدِيثي مَعَ اَلنَّاسِ ؟
‘Omar: “With (all) pleasure	عُمَرُ : بِكُلِّ سُرُورٍ
(and) what would you like (as) an example?”	وَمَاذَا تُرِيدُ مَثَلاً ؟
Charles: “I want to know	شَارْل : أُرِيدُ أَنْ أَعْرِفَ
the morning greeting.”	تَحِيَّةَ اَلصَّبَاح
‘Omar: “The morning greeting (it) is	عُمَرُ : تَحِيَّةُ اَلصَّبَاحِ هِيَ :
‘Good morning’ (morning of goodness)”	صَبَاحُ اَلْخَيْرِ
Charles: “(and) what is the evening greeting?”	شَارْل : وَمَا هِيَ تَحِيَّةُ اَلْمَسَاءِ ؟

'Omar: "The greeting of the evening (it) is	عُمَرُ : تَحِيَّةُ ٱلْمَسَاءِ هِيَ
'Good Evening' (evening of goodness)."	«مَسَاءُ ٱلْخَيْرِ !»
Charles: "Is there a greeting valid	شَارْل : هَلْ هُنَاكَ تَحِيَّةٌ صَالِحَةٌ
for any time (of day)?"	لِكُلِّ وَقْتٍ
'Omar: "Yes! There is	عُمَرُ : نَعَمْ ! هُنَاكَ
a greeting valid for any time (of day),	تَحِيَّةٌ صَالِحَةٌ لِكُلِ وَقْتٍ
and it (is) - 'Peace be upon you!'	وَهِيَ : «السَّلَامُ عَلَيْكُمْ !»
and its answer (is):	وَجَوَابُهَا :
'Upon you be peace and	«عَلَيْكُمُ السَّلَامُ وَ
the mercy of God and His blessings.' "	رَحْمَةُ اللّٰهِ وَبَرَكَاتُهُ»
Charles: "Many thanks	شَارْل : شُكْراً جَزِيلاً
for these instructions	عَلَى هَذِهِ ٱلْمَعْلُومَاتِ
and this (is) enough (for) today,	وَيَكْفِي هَذَا ٱلْيَوْمَ
and will you allow (for) me to leave?"	وَهَلْ تَسْمَحُ لِي بِالانْصِرَافِ ؟
'Omar: "Please do! (be bountiful, have the goodness)	عُمَرُ : تَفَضَّلْ !
with (all) pleasure."	بِكُلِّ سُرُورٍ
Charles: (shaking 'Omar's hand)	شَارْل (مُصَافِحاً عُمَرَ)
"Peace be upon you!	اَلسَّلَامُ عَلَيْكُمْ !

Upon you be peace, and	عُمَرُ : عَلَيْكُمُ السَّلامُ وَ
the mercy of Allah and His blessings	رَحْمَةُ اللَّهِ وَبَرَكَاتُهُ
in the keeping of Allah ! (good-bye)"	فِي أَمَانِ اللَّهِ !

Exercise

تَمْرِينٌ

1. Why did 'Omar come to London?	١ – لِمَاذَا حَضَرَ عُمَرُ الى لَنْدَنَ ؟
2. What did Charles study?	٢ – مَاذَا كَانَ يَدْرُسُ شَارْلُ ؟
3. Is Charles an Egyptian youth?	٣ – شَارْل ، هَلْ هُوَ شَابٌ مِصْرِيٌّ ؟
4. Is 'Omar an Egyptian youth?	٤ – عُمَرَ ، هَلْ هُوَ شَابٌ اِنْجليزيٌّ ؟
5. Why did Charles wish to visit Egypt?	٥ – لِمَاذَا أَرَادَ شَارْلُ أَنْ يَزُورَ مِصْرَ ؟
6. What is the greeting of the morning?	٦ – مَا هِيَ تَحِيَّةُ الصَّباحِ ؟
7. What is the greeting of the evening?	٧ – مَا هِيَ تَحِيَّةُ المَسَاءِ ؟
8. What is the valid greeting for any time of day?	٨ – مَا هِيَ التَّحِيَّةُ الصَّالِحَةُ لِكُلِّ وَقْتٍ ؟
9. What did Charles say (while he was) shaking Omar's hand?	٩ – مَاذَا قَالَ شَارْل مُصَافِحاً عُمَرَ ؟
10. What did 'Omar say to Charles (in reply)?	١٠ – مَاذَا قَالَ عُمَرُ لِشَارْل (مُجِيباً) ؟

٢ صَبَاحُ اَلْخَيْرِ !

2. Good Morning!

"Good morning, (oh) 'Omar!"	صَبَاحُ اَلْخَيْرِ يَا عُمَرُ !
"Good morning, (oh) Charles!"	«صَبَاحُ اَلْخَيْرِ يَا شَارْل !»
"How are you today?"	«كَيْفَ حَالُكَ اَلْيَوم ؟»
'Omar: "Well (with goodness) and praise be to Allah."	عُمَرُ : «بِخَيْرٍ وَ اَلْحَمْدُ لِلّٰهِ»
Charles: "The weather is beautiful!"	شَارْل : «اَلْجَوُّ جَمِيلٌ !»
'Omar: "Very beautiful!"	عُمَرُ : «جَمِيلٌ جِداً !»
Charles: "Are you going to the faculty?"	شَارْل : أَنْتَ ذَاهِبٌ الىَ الكُلِّيةِ ؟»
'Omar: "Yes! I am going to the faculty."	عُمَر : نَعَمْ ! أَنَا ذَاهِبٌ الىَ الكُلِّيَّةِ»
Charles: "Then I will accompany you!"	شَارْل : إِذَنْ أَصْحَبُكَ !»
'Omar: "I will be very happy (if you do)."	عُمَر : «أَكُونُ سَعِيداً جِداً»

٣ «آسِفٌ !»

3. "I am sorry!"

Charles: "I am sorry, I am five	شَارْل : «آسِفٌ تَأَخَّرْتُ خَمْسَ
minutes late for my appointment."	دَقَائِق عَنْ مَوْعِدِي»
'Omar: "Good (Inshā'Allah) God	عُمَرُ : خَيْراً (إِنْ شَاءَ اللّه)
willing; what happened?"	مَاذا حَدَثَ ؟
Charles: "The bus was (arrived) late."	شَارْل : «(الأوتوبيس) وَصَلَ مُتَأَخِراً»
'Omar: "Well (good happened), and now	عُمَر : «(جَرَى خَيْرٌ) وَالآن
(would) you like a cup of coffee?"	تُحِبُّ فِنْجَانَ قَهْوَة ؟»
Charles: "Thanks, I'd like that	شَارْل : «شُكراً ، أُحِبُّ ذَلِكَ
(very) much."	كَثِيراً
'Omar: "Coffee with or without sugar?"	عُمَرُ : قَهْوَةَ سَادَةٍ أَو بِسُكَر ؟»
Charles: "With sugar and milk please	شَارْل : بِسُكَر وَلَبَنٍ ، (مِنْ فَضْلِكَ)»
(out of your bounty)."	
'Omar calls the servant:	عُمَرُ يُنَادِي الْخَادِمَ :
"Please, a cup of coffee with sugar and	«مِنْ فَضْلِكَ ، فِنْجَان قَهْوَة بِسُكَّرٍ و
milk for Mr Charles,	وَلُبَنٍ لِلسَّيِّدِ شَارْل»

and an ordinary cup without milk for me.	وَفِنْجان سَادَةٍ مِنْ غَيْرِ لَبَنٍ لِي»
Please (I beg you to) hurry because	(أَرْجُوكَ) أَن تُسْرِعَ لأَنِّي
I am going with Mr Charles to the zoo	ذاهِبٌ مَعَ اَلْسَيِّد شَارْل الى
(the garden of animals) in five minutes time."	(حَدِيقَةِ اَلْحَيَوان) بَعْدَ خَمْس دقَائق .
The Servant: "Soon! (oh my) master!"	اَلْخَادِمُ : «حَالاً ! يَا سَيِّدي !»

٤ مَسَاءُ اَلْخَيْر

4. Good Evening!

تَقَابَلَ شَارْلُ وَعُمَرُ عِنْدَ مَحَطَّةِ (الأوتُوبِيس)

(Charles and 'Omar met each other at the bus-stop.)

C: "Good evening! (evening of goodness)"	ش : (مَسَاءُ اَلْخَيْرِ !)
O: "Good evening!"	ع : «مَسَاءُ اَلْخَيْر !»
C: "Who is this lady?"	ش : «مَنْ هَذِهِ اَلْسَيِّدَةُ ؟»
O: "This lady is my mother	ع : «هَذِهِ السَّيِّدَةُ وَالِدَتي
and her name (is) (Najlāu)."	وَاسْمُهَا (نَجْلاءُ)
C: "And who is this gentleman (master)?"	ش : «وَمَنْ هَذَا اَلْسَيِّدُ ؟»
O: "This gentleman is my father	ع : «هَذَا اَلْسَيِّدُ وَالِدِي
and his name (is) (Raū'f)."	وَاسْمُهُ رَؤُوفٌ»

C: "It is a great honour	ش : «هَذَا شَرَفٌ عَظِيمٌ !»
(to meet you)!"	
O: "Where are you going?"	ع : «أَيْنَ تَذْهَبُ ؟»
C: "I am going to (Enfield Town)	ش : «أَنَا ذَاهِبٌ الى (مَدينة انْفِيلد)
in (the) North (of) London to visit	فِي شَمَالِي لَنْدَن لِزِيَارَةِ
my sister where she lives. And you?"	أُخْتِي حَيْثُ تَسْكُنُ ، وَأَنْتَ ؟»
O: "I am going with my father and	ع : «أَنَا ذَاهِبٌ مَعَ وَالِدي وَ
(my) mother to visit my uncle	وَالِدَتِي لِزِيَارَةِ عَمِّي
and he lives in (the) South (of) London.	وَهُوَ يَسْكُنُ فِي جَنُوبِيِّ لَنْدَن
I am going by train.	أَنَا ذَاهِبٌ بِالْقِطَارِ
With your permission . . .	عَنْ إِذْنِك !
Peace be upon you!"	السَّلامُ عَلَيْكُم ؟»
C: "Upon you be peace! Good-bye!	ش : عَلَيْكُم السَّلامُ
(safety be with you)."	(مَعَ السَّلامَةِ !)

٥ . دَعْوَةٌ اِاى الشَّــاى .

5. An Invitation to Tea

(Charles invited his friend ‘Omar	دَعَا شَارْلُ صَدِيقَهُ عُمَرَ
to have tea at his house	إلى تَنَاوِلِ الشَّاي بِمَنْزِله
at 5.00 pm on Monday.	فِي السَّاعَةِ الخَامسةِ مَسَاءً يَوْمَ الأثْنَين
‘Omar went to the house at the fixed	ذَهَبَ عُمَرُ إِلَى المَنْزِلِ فِي المَوْعد
appointment and rang the bell.)	اَلْمُحَدَّدِ وَدَقَّ اَلْجَرَسَ .
Charles opens the door, saying:	-شَارْلُ يَفْتحْ اَلبَابَ قَائلاً :
“Hello! ‘Omar!” (you are with parents and at home)	(أهْلًا وَسَهْلًا) يَاعُمَرْ
“Hello!” (I am with parents by virtue of you)	-(أَهْلًا بِكَ !)
C: “Please (be bountiful), come in!	ش :(تَفَضَّلْ !) أُدْخُلْ !
This is my sister, Mary.”	هَذِهِ أُخْتِي مَارِية
M: “Hello!”	م : أَهْلًا وسَهْلًا
O: “I have the honour (to know you).”	ع : تَشَرَّفْتُ
C: “And this is my brother, George.”	ش : هَذَا أَخِي جُورْج
G: “Hello!”	ج : أَهْلًا وَسهْلًا

O: "I have the honour."	ع : تَشَرَّفْتُ
(They all sat down around the table.)	(جَلَسُوا جَمِيعًا حَوْلَ ٱلْمَائِدَةِ .)
"Do you like (your) tea strong (heavy)?"	– هَلْ تُحِبُّ الشَّاىَ (ثَقِيلًا) ؟
O: "I like it weak (light), please."	ع : أُحِبُّهُ خَفِيفًا ، مِنْ فَضْلِكَ !
"How much (many spoons of) sugar?"	–كَمْ مِلْعَقَةً مِنَ السُّكَّرِ ؟
O: "Two, please!"	ع : اثْنَتَانِ ، مِنْ فَضْلِكَ !
"What (would) you like with tea?"	– مَاذَا تُحِبُّ مَعَ الشَّاىِ ؟
O: "I (would) like a cheese and	ع : أُحِبُّ (سَانْدوِتْشًا) مِنَ ٱلْجُبْنِ و
cucumber sandwich, and some cakes,	الخِيَار وَبَعْضًا مِن ٱلْكَعْكِ
and some biscuits."	وَبَعْضًا مِنَ (ٱلْبِسْكَوِيتِ)
"Take what you like,	– تَنَاوَلْ مَاتُرِيدُ
everything is at (under) your disposal.	كُلُّ شَىْءٍ تَحتَ أَمْرِك
Would you like another cup of (the) tea?"	–تُحِبُّ فِنْجَانًا آخَرَ مِنَ الشَّاىِ
O: "Yes, please!"	ع : نَعَمْ ! مِنْ فَضْلِكَ !
(And they exchanged conversation happily.)	(وَتَبادَلُوا ٱلْحَدِيثَ مَسْرُورِينَ)
At six o'clock ('Omar) asks permission	فِى السَّاعَةِ السَّادِسَةِ اسْتَأْذَنَ عُمَرُ
to leave, saying:	الانْصِرَاف قَائِلًا :
"I invite you to have tea with me	انَّنِى أَدْعُوكُم لِتَنَاوُلِ الشَّاىَ مَعِى
next Monday."	يوم الاِثْنَيْنِ القادِمِ

C: "Thanks, this will please us very much!" (it will be a pleasure)	ش : شُكْرًا ، إنَّ ذَلِكَ يَسُرُّنا كثيرًا جدًا .
C: "In this connection,	ش : «بِهَذِهِ المُنَاسَبَةِ ،
(I beg you to give me) may I have	(أَرْجُوكَ أَنْ تُعْطِيَنِي)
your new address and (your new)	عُنْوَانَكَ اَلْجَدِيد و
telephone number?"	رَقْمَ تِلِيفُونك (اَلْجَدِيدَ)
O: "The new address (it) is -	ع : «اَلْعُنْوانُ الجَدِيدُ هُوَ :
55 King Street, London	٥٥ شَارِعُ اَلْمَلِكِ لَنْدَن
and the 'phone no. 111-2233."	وَرَقْمُ التِّلِيفُون ٢٢٣٣ – ١١١
C: "Thank you."	ش : شُكْرًا !
O: "And now, peace be upon you."	ع : «وَالآنَ ، السَّلَامُ عَلَيْكُمْ !»
C: "And upon you be peace."	ش : «وَعَلَيْكُمُ السَّلَامُ !»
"Good-bye!" (safety be with you)	(مَعَ السَّلَامَةِ)

٦ – اَلْيَـوْمُ –

6. The Day

Charles: "Tell me about time	ش : «أَخْبِرْنِي عَنِ الوَقْتِ
in Arabic."	بِالْعَرَبِيَّةِ»
'Omar: "I will tell you (firstly)	ع : أُخْبِرُكَ أَوَّلًا
about the day.	عَنِ اليَوْمِ .
The day (has) 24 hours,	اَلْيَوْمُ أَرْبَعٌ وعُشْرُونَ سَاعَةً .
one (the) hour (has) 60 minutes,	السَّاعَةُ سِتُّونَ دَقِيقَةً .
one (the) minute (has) 60 seconds.	الدَّقِيقَةُ سِتُّونَ ثَانِيةً .
The time from (the) sunrise to sunset	الوَقْتُ مِنْ شُرُوقِ الشَّمْسِ
to sunset is day-time.	إِلَى غُرُوبِ الشمس ، نَهَارٌ .
the time from sunset	اَلْوَقْتُ مِنْ غُرُوبِ الشَّمْسِ
to its rise is night-time.	إِلَى شُرُوقِهَا ، لَيْلٌ .
The beginning of the day (time) is the morning,	أَوَّل النَّهَارِ الصُّبْحُ .
the end of the day (time) is the sunset,	أَخِرُ النَّهَارِ المَغْرِبُ
(the) noon is the middle of the day (time)	الظُّهْرُ مُنْتَصَفُ النَّهَارِ .
The forenoon is between the morning and noon,	الضُّحَى مَابَيْنَ الصُّبْحِ والظُّهْرِ .
the afternoon is between noon and sunset.	العَصْرُ مَابَيْنَ الظُّهْرِ وَالمَغْرِبِ .

٧ – الأُسْبُوعُ

7. The Week

“The week has seven days,	«الأُسْبُوعُ سَبْعَةُ أَيَّامٍ
the days of the week are:	أَيَّامُ الأُسْبُوعِ هى :
Saturday	١ . يَوْمُ السَّبْتِ
Sunday	٢ . " الأَحَدِ
Monday	٣ . " الأَثْنَيْنِ
Tuesday	٤ . " الثُّلاثاء
Wednesday	٥ . " الأَرْبعاء
Thursday	٦ . " اَلخَمِيسِ
Friday	٧ . " الجُمُعَةِ
Saturday is the day of rest	يَوْمُ السَبْتِ يَوْمُ الرَّاحَةِ
for the Jews;	عِنْدَ اَلْيَهُودِ .
Sunday is the day of rest	يَوْمُ الأَحَدِ يَوْمُ الرَّاحَةِ
for the Christians.	عِنْدَ النَّصَارَى
Friday is the day of the congregational	يَوْمُ الجُمُعَةِ يَوْمُ صَلاَة اَلجَمَاعَةِ ،
prayer, without rest, for the Muslims.”	بلاَ رَاحَةِ ، عِنْدَ المُسْلِمِينَ .»

٨ شُهُور السَّنَةِ الْمِيلاَدِيَّةِ

8. Months of the Christian Year*

"Months of the Christian year (they) are	شُهُورُ السَّنَةِ المِيلادِيَّةِ هِيَ :
January	١ يَنَايِر
February	٢ فِبْرَايِر
March	٣ مَارِس
April	٤ أَبْرِيل
May	٥ مَايُو
June	٦ يُونيه – يُونْيُو
July	٧ يُولْيَه – يُولْيُو
August	٨ اَغُسْطُس
September	٩ سبْتَمْبِر
October	١٠ أُكْتُوبر
November	١١ نُوفَمبِر
December	١٢ دِيسَمْبِر

*The Christian Year is called (السَّنَةُ المِيلادية), the birth year.
Dates B.C. are called (قَبْلَ المِيلادِ – ق.م)

Dates A.D. are called (بَعْدَ المِيلادِ – ب.م) or, simply: (م)

٩ شُهُورُ السَّنَةِ اَلْهِجْرِيَّةِ

9. The Muslim Year*

Charles: "Thank you (very) much; — شَارِل : أَشْكُرُكَ كَثِيراً

and what are the months of the Islamic year?" — ومَا هِيَ شُهُورُ اَلسَّنَةِ الاسلامِيَّةِ؟

'Omar: "The months of the Islamic year — عُمَرْ : شُهُورُ اَلسَّنَةِ الاسلامِيَّة

(they) are: — هِـيَ :

١ اَلْمُحَرَّمُ

٢ صَفَرٌ

٣ رَبِيعُ الأَوَّل

٤ رَبِيعُ الثَّانِي

٥ جُمَادَى الأُولَى

٦ جُمَادَى الثَّانِيَة

٧ رَجَبٌ

٨ شَعْبَانُ

٩ رَمَضَـــانُ (شَهــرُ الصَّومِ)

(fasting month)

١٠ شَوَّالٌ

١١ ذو اَلْقِعْدَةِ

١٢ ذُو اَلْحِجَّةِ (شَهْرُ الحَجِّ)

(pilgrimage month)

*It is called the هِجْرَة Flight of the Prophet Muḥammad from Makka to Medina on the 16th July, 622 A.D. Dates have the letter (هـ) after them.

Stories and Tales

قِصَصٌ وَحِكَايَاتٌ

أَنْتَ عَلَى حَقٍّ !

"You are right!?"

Ibrahīm and Alī quarrelled;	تَشَاجَر ابْراهيمُ وَعَليٌّ ،
then, Ibrahīm went to the judge	فَذَهَبَ ابْراهِيمُ الَى القَاضِي ،
and told him what had happened.	وَقَصَّ عَلَيْهِ مَا حَدَث .
So, the judge looked at him and said:	فَنَظَرَ إلَيْهِ القَاضِي وَقال :
"You are right!"	«أَنْتَ عَلَى حَقٍّ !»
And then Alī went to the judge,	ثُمَّ ذَهَبَ عَليٌّ الى القَاضِي ،
and told him what had happened.	وَقَصَّ عَلَيْهِ مَا حَدَث .
So, the judge looked at him and said:	فَنَظَرَ إلَيْهِ القَاضِي وَقَال :
"You are right!"	«أَنْتَ عَلَى حَقٍّ !»
The wife of the judge was	كَانَتْ زَوْجَةُ القَاضِي
behind a curtain.	وَرَاءَ سِتَار
So, she went to her husband and said:	فَذَهَبَتْ الَى زَوْجِهَا وَقَالَت :
"Ibrahīm came to you and you said –	جَاءَ ابْراهِيمُ وَقُلْتُ :

'You are right!	«أَنْتَ عَلَى حَقٍّ ! »
and then Alī came to you and you said -	ثُمَّ جاءَ عَليٌّ وَقُلْتَ :
'You are right!"	«أَنْتَ عَلَى حَقٍّ ! »
So, then, where is (will be) the truth?"	فَأَيْنَ إذَنْ يَكُونُ الحَقُّ ؟
The judge looked at her and said -	فَنَظَرَ اليْهَا الْقَاضِي وَقَالَ :
"You are right!"	«انْتِ عَلَى حَقٍّ ! »

غَـايَـةٌ لاَ تُنَـالُ !

"An unattainable aim!"

One day Goḥā went to the market;*	يَوْماً ذَهَبَ «جُحَا» إلى السُّوقِ ،
he rode his donkey and took	رَكِبَ حِمَارَه وَاخَذَ
his son behind him.	ابْنَهُ وَرَاءَهُ
Then he passed by a group (of people)	فَمَرَّ عَلَى جَمَاعَةٍ
and he heard them saying:	وَسَمِعَهُم يَقُولُونَ :

*Goḥā (جُحَا) is an imaginary personality to whom the people usually ascribe the sayings, stories etc. to express their popular wisdom, criticism, emotions and all sorts of suppressions.

"How cruel!	«يَا لَلْقَسْوَة !
He and his son ride	يَرْكَبُ هُوَ وَابْنُهُ
on one donkey."	عَلَى حِمَار وَاحِدٍ»
So, Goḥā descended and left	فَنَزَلَ «جُحًا» وَتَرَكَ
his son alone on the donkey	إبْنَهُ وَحْدَهُ عَلَى الْحِمَارِ
and passed by another group	وَمَرَّ عَلَى جمَاعةٍ أُخْرَى
and he heard them saying:	وَسَمِعَهُم يقُولُونَ :
"What a fool!	«يَالَه مِنْ غَبِيٍّ !
He walks behind his son and	يَسِيرُ وَرَاءَ ابْنِهِ وَ
leaves him riding the donkey alone."	يَدَعُهُ يرْكَبُ الحِمَارَ وحْدَهُ»
So, he lets his son get down	فَأَنْزَلَ ابْنَهُ
and (he) took his place,	وَأَخذَ مكَانَهُ
and his son walked behind the donkey.	وَسَارَ ابنُهُ وَرَاءَ الحِمَارِ .
He passed by yet another group	ومَرَّ عَلَى جمَاعةٍ أُخْرَى
and he heard them saying:	وَسَمِعَهُم يقُولُونَ :
"A ruthless man!	«رَجُلٌ بلاَ رَحْمَةٍ
He rides and lets his son	يَرْكَبُ وَيَدَعُ ابْنَهُ
walk behind him."	يَسِيرُ وَرَاءَهُ »
So, Goḥā descended and walked	فَنَزَلَ «جُحا» وَسَارَ

with his son behind the donkey.	مَعَ ابْنِهِ وَرَاءَ الحِمَارِ ،
He passed by yet another group	وَمَرَّ بِجَمَاعَةٍ أُخْرَى
and heard them saying:	وَسَمِعَهُم يَقُولُونَ :
"What a mad man!	«يَا لَهُ مِنْ رَجُلٍ مَجْنونٍ !
He walks with his son	يَسِيرُ هُوَ وَابْنُهُ
behind the donkey	وَرَاءَ الحِمَارِ
and leaves the donkey	وَيَتْرُكُ الحِمَارَ
not to carry either (of them)."	لاَ يَحْمِلُ أَحَداً» .
Here Goḥā stopped	هُنَا تَوَقَّفَ «جُحَا»
- perplexed! wondering! -	مُتَحَيِّراً ! مُتَعَجِّباً !
and said: "Oh, my son!	وَقَالَ : «يَا وَلَدِي !
To please all the people	أَنْ تُرْضِيَ النَّاسَ جَمِيعاً
is an unattainable aim!"	غَايَةٌ لاَ تُنَالُ !» .

أَسَدٌ وَثَعْلَبٌ وَذِئْبٌ

A Lion, a Fox and a Wolf

A lion went out in search of food	خَرَجَ اَسَدٌ في طَلَبِ القُوتِ
and with him (were) a fox and a wolf.	وَمَعَهُ ثَعْلَبٌ وَذِئْبٌ
then, they caught a zebra (lit. a wild donkey)	فَاصْطَادُوا حِمَارَاً وَحْشِيّاً
a gazelle and a rabbit	وَغَزَالاً وَأَرْنَباً
(And) when they returned	فَلَمَّا رَجَعُوا
the lion said to the wolf:	قَالَ الأَسَدُ لِلْذِئْبِ :
"Divide (them) amongst us,"	«أَقْسِمْ بَيْنَنَا»
then the wolf said:	فَقَالَ الذِّئْبُ :
"The zebra (is) for the king (of the forest)	«حِمَارُ الوَحْشِ لِلْمَلِكِ ،
and the gazelle (is) for the fox	وَالغَزَالُ لِلثَعْلَبِ ،
and the rabbit (is) for me."	وَالأَرْنَبُ لِي .»
So, the lion caught him by his leg	فَأَمْسَكَهُ الأَسَدُ مِنْ سَاقِهِ
and nearly pulled it off,	وَكَادَ أَنْ يَفْصِلَهَا
and then he said to the fox:	ثُمَّ قَالَ لَلْثَعْلَبِ :
"Divide (them)!"	«أَقْسِمْ !»

So, the fox said:	فقالَ الثّعْلَبُ :
"The judgement is clear! -	«اَلْحُكْمُ وَاضِحٌ !
the zebra (is) for the king	حِمَارُ اَلْوَحْشِ لِلْمَلِكِ
to dine on (it),	يَتَغَذّى بهِ ،
and the gazelle (is) for the king	وَالغزَالُ لِلْمَلِكِ
to breakfast on (it),	يُفْطِرُ بهِ ،
and the rabbit (is) for the king	وَالأرْنَبُ لِلْمَلِكِ
in between (that) to relish (it)."	فِيمَا بَيْنَ ذَلِكَ يَتعَلَّلُ بهِ .»
The lion was pleased and said:	فَسُرَّ الأسَدُ وَقَالَ :
"What a fair judge, oh fox!	«مَا أَقْضَاكَ يَا ثَعْلَبُ !
Who has taught you (this) judgement?"	مَنْ عَلَّمَكَ القَضَاءَ ؟»
The fox said:	قَالَ الثَّعْلَبُ :
"The leg of the wolf taught me,	«عَلَّمَتْنِي سَاقُ الذِّئْبِ
oh my Lord!"	يَا مَوْلاَيَ !»

Exercise تَمْـرِيـن

أَجِبْ :

1. ١ – كَيْفَ قَسمَ الذِّئْبُ ؟
2. ٢ – كَيْفَ قَسمَ الثَّعْلَبُ ؟

3. Write three lines explaining the message of the story.

الفَـلاحُ وَ الهُـدْهُـدُ

The Farmer and the Hoopoe

One day the farmer went to his field	ذَهَبَ الفَلاح يَوْماً إلى حَقلِهِ
and he found the crows	فَوَجَدَ الغِرِبَانَ
eating his corn.	تأكُلُ قَمْحَهُ
So, he was very sad (and) when	فَحزِنَ كَثِيراً وَلَمَّا
he went back to his house	عَادَ إلى بَيْتِهِ
his wife saw him sad.	رَأَتْهُ زَوْجَتُهُ حَزِيناً
She asked him the reason for his sadness	فَسأَلَتْهُ عَنْ سَبَبِ حُزْنِهِ
(and) he said to her:	فَقَالَ لَهَا :
"Surely, the crows are eating the corn,	«إنَّ الغِرِبَانَ تَأكُلُ القَمْحَ
and if I leave them they will	وإذَا تَرْكْتُهَا
finish off the entire crop."	قَضَتْ عَلَى المَحْصُولِ كُلِّهِ .»
His wife was a wise woman	كَانَتْ زَوجَتُهُ سَيِّدَةً عَاقِلَةً
and she said to him:	فَقَالَتْ لَهُ :
"Do not be sad; let us	«لاَ تَحْزَن وَهَيَّا بِنَا
have (our) the supper	نَتَنَاوَلُ العَشَاءَ
and then (we) go to (the) bed,	ثُمَّ نَذْهَبُ إلَى الفِرَاشِ ،

and (we) sleep peacefully	وَنَنَامُ هَادِئَيْنِ ،
(and) hoping in the morning	وَلَعَلَّ فِي الصَّبَاحِ
we will find a solution."	نَجِدُ حَلاًّ . »
Her words pleased him	فَسَرَّهُ كَلامُهَا
(and) he slept with a quiet mind.	وَنَامَ هَادِئَ البَالِ .
In the morning,	فِي الصَّبَاحِ
after they had had (the) breakfast	بَعْدَ أن تَنَاوَلا الإفْطَارَ
his wife said to him:	قَالَت لَهُ زَوْجَتُهُ
"I thought over	«فَكَرْتُ في
the question of the crows	مَسْأَلَةِ الغِرْبَانِ
(but) I did not find a solution	وَلَمْ أَجِدْ حَلاًّ
to this problem other (better) than	لِهَذِهِ المُشْكِلَةِ خَيْراً مِنْ
fixing a net for them	أَنْ نَنْصِبَ شَبَكَةً لَهَا
in the centre of the threshing floor;	فِي وَسَطِ الجُرْنِ ،
(then) if they come	فَإذَا جَاءَتْ
they will fall in the net."	وَقَعَتْ فِي الشَّبَكَةِ . »
So the farmer followed her advice	فَتَبِعَ الفَلاَّحُ نَصِيحَتَهَا ،
and after two days	وَبَعْدَ يَوْمَيْنِ ،
he found the net had caught	وَجَدَ الشَّبَكَةَ قَدْ أَمْسَكَتْ

all the crows.	بِالغرْبَانِ كُلِّهَا .
He began to kill them	فَأخذَ يَذْبَحُهَا
one by one;	وَاحِداً وَاحِداً
(but) among them was	وَكَانَ بينَهَا
a peaceable hoopoe.	هُدْهُدٌ وَدِيعٌ
The farmer was about to kill it	اَوْشَكَ الفَلاَّحُ أنْ يَقْتُلَهُ ،
so the hoopoe cried and said:	فَبَكَى الهُدهُدُ وَقَالَ :
"Do me a favour,	«اعْمَلْ فِيَّ مَعْرُوفاً ،
and let me (live) this time,	وَدَعْنِي هَذِهِ المَرَّةَ
because I am a good and honest bird."	لأَنِّي طَائِرٌ طَيِّبٌ وَأَمِينٌ .»
The farmer was touched	فَتَأَثَّرَ الفَلاَّحُ
by his words, and said:	بِكَلاَمِهِ وَقَالَ :
"I will forgive you this time,	«أُسَامِحُكَ هَذِهِ المَرَّةَ
but you must know that he who mixes	وَلَكِنِ أعْلَمْ أَنَّ مَنْ يُخَالِط
with the wicked (he) will be treated	الأَشْرَارَ لاَ بُدَّ أَنْ يُعَامَلَ
as they (are). So, do not mix with	مِثْلَهُم . فَلا تُخَالِطِ
the wicked again," and set it free.	الأَشْرَارَ ثَانِيةً . وأَطْلَقَ سَرَاحَهُ .

تَمْـرِينٌ Exercise

أجِبْ :-

١ – لِمَاذَا حَزِنَ الفلاَّحُ ؟

٢ – مَاذَا قَالَ الهُدْهُدُ لِلْفَلاَّحِ ؟

٣ – مَا مَغْزَى (morale) هَذِهِ القِصَّةِ ؟

حِكَمٌ وَأَمْثَالٌ

Proverbs and Aphorisms

Proverbs and aphorisms are common and popular forms to express the wisdom, experiences, practices and values of life in the eyes of the people, in every language.

Here are examples of this form of speech in which you will notice that the translation is almost literal. The English equivalent is stated in brackets to show the similarity between the two viewpoints.

1. * ١ إِيشْ يَأْخُذُ الرِّيحُ مِنَ الْبَلَاطِ

What can the wind take from floor-tiles?
(Where there is nothing, the king loses his rights.)

2. ٢ أَنَا أَمِيرٌ وَأَنْتَ أَمِيرٌ، مَنْ يَسُوقُ الْحَمِيرَ

I am a prince and you are a prince,
who will drive the donkey?
(There is no accord where every man would be a lord.)

3. ٣ الشَّاطِرَةُ تَغزِل بِرِجْلِ حِمَارٍ

The clever girl spins with the leg of a donkey.
(A good workman does not quarrel with his tools.)

4. ٤ إِنْ دَخَلَتَ بَلَداً تَعْبُدُ العِجْلَ حِشْ وَأَطْعِمهُ

If you enter a city worshipping a calf,
mow grass and feed him.
(When in Rome, do as the Romans do.)

* إيش is an abbreviation of أَيُّ شَيْءٍ which literally means 'what thing?'

5 ٥ بَابُ النَّجارِ (تَمَلِّي) مُخَلَّع

The carpenter's door is always badly hung.
(The cobbler's wife is always the worst shod.)

6. ٦ الغَايِبُ حُجَّتُهُ مَعَهُ.

The absent has his excuse.
(The absent party is not so faulty.)

7. ٧ التَّكْرَارُ يُعَلِّمُ الحِمَارَ

Repetition teaches the donkey.
(Practice makes perfect.)

8. ٨ بَيْضَةُ اليَوْمِ وَلا فَرْخَةُ بُكْرَة

The egg of today and not the hen of tomorrow.
(A bird in the hand is worth two in the bush.)

9. ٩ لَمَّا تَقَعُ البَقَرَةُ تَكْثُرُ السَّكَاكِينُ

When the cow falls down, knives are plentiful.
(When a man is going downhill, everybody gives him a kick.)

10. ١٠ كَلامُ اللَّيْلِ مَدْهُونٌ بِزُبدَة يَطْلَعُ عَلَيْهِ النَّهَارُ يَسِيحُ

The words of the night are coated with butter; as soon as the day shines upon them, they melt away.
(Words spoken in the evening, the wind carries away.)

11. ١١ إذَا تَخَاصَمَ اللِّصَّانِ ظَهَرَ المَسْرُوقُ

When two thieves quarrel, the stolen thing is visible.
(When rogues fall out, honest men come by their own.)

12. ١٢ فَقْرٌ بِلاَ دَيْنٌ هُوَ الغِنَى التَّامُ

Poverty without debt is real richness.
(He that gets out of debt grows rich.)

13. ١٣ حَبِيبُكَ يَمْضُغُ لَكَ الزَّلَطَ وَعَدُوُّكَ يَعُدُّ لكَ الغَلَط

Your friend chews pebbles for you, and your enemy counts your mistakes.
(When love fails, we spy all faults.)

14. ١٤ أَبُو جُعْرَان فِي بَيْتِهِ سُلْطَانٌ

The beetle in its hole is a sultan.
(Every cock is a king on his own dunghill.)

15. ١٥ رَئِيسَانِ فِي المَرْكِبِ تَغْرقُ

Two pilots in the boat and it will sink.
(Too many cooks spoil the broth.)

16. ١٦ عِنْدَ البُطُونِ تَضِيعُ العُقُولُ

When the stomachs are concerned, wits are lost.
(An empty belly hears nobody.)

17. ١٧ عَذَابُ سَاعَةٍ وَلاَ كُلُّ سَاعَة

Suffering for an hour but not suffering for every day.
(Better eye out than always aching.)

18. ١٨ إنْ كُنْتَ كَذُوباً فَكُن ذَكُوراً

If you are a liar, then have a good memory.
(Liars should have good memories.)

19. ١٩ ضَحِكٌ مِنْ غَيْرِ سَبَبٍ قِلَّةُ أَدَبٍ

A laugh without reason shows lack of tact.
(The loud laugh bespeaks the vacant mind.)

20. ٢٠ القِرِدُ فِي عَيْنِ أُمِّهِ غزَالٌ

The monkey in his mother's eye is a gazelle.
(Every mother thinks her own goose a swan.)

21. ٢١ العَجَلَةُ مِنَ الشَّيْطَانِ

Haste is of the devil.
(More haste, less speed.)

22. ٢٢ رَأْسُ الكَسْلاَنِ بَيْتُ الشَّيْطَانِ

The head of the idle is the house of Satan.
(Satan finds some mischief still for idle hands to do.)

23. ٢٣ لَبِّسْ البوصَة تَبْقَى عَرُوسَةً

Dress the reed and it will resemble the bride.
(Fine feathers make find birds.)

24. **٢٤ الأَكْلُ في الشَّبْعَانِ خُسَارَةٌ**

To feed a satiated person is a waste.
(It is idle to bestow alms where there is no need.)

عَلامَاتُ التَّرْقِيمِ

Punctuation Marks

Punctuation marks in modern Arabic are like the European, with some slight alterations, e.g.

English Name	Arabic Name	Symbol
Comma	فَصْلَةٌ = فَاصِلَةٌ = شَوْلَة	،
Semi-colon	فَصْلَةٌ مَنْقُوطَةٌ	؛
Colon	نُقْطَتَانِ	:
Full-stop	نُقْطَةٌ نِهَائِيَّةٌ	.
Quotation Marks	عَلامَةُ التَّنْصِيصِ	« »
Brackets	قَوْسَانِ	( )
Question Mark	عَلامَةُ اسْتِفْهَامٍ	؟
Exclamation Mark	عَلامَةُ تَعَجُّبٍ	!
Dash	شَرْطَةٌ	–

أَبْجَدِيَّة العَدَد

Numerical Values of the Arabic Alphabet

مَائَتَيْنِ	200	٢٠٠	ر	عِشْرِينَ	20	٢٠	ك	وَاحِداً	1	١	أ
ثَلْثَمِائَةٍ	300	٣٠٠	ش	ثَلاثِين	30	٣٠	ل	اثْنَيْنِ	2	٢	ب
أَرْبَعمائَةٍ	400	٤٠٠	ت	أَرْبَعِينَ	40	٤٠	م	ثَلاثَةً	3	٣	ج
خَمْسَمَائَةٍ	500	٥٠٠	ث	خَمْسِينَ	50	٥٠	ن	أَرْبَعَةً	4	٤	د
سِتَّمائَةٍ	600	٦٠٠	خ	سِتين	60	٦٠	س	خَمْسَةً	5	٥	هـ
سَبْعَمائَةٍ	700	٧٠٠	ذ	سَبْعِينَ	70	٧٠	ع	سِتَّة	6	٦	و
ثَمانِمائَةٍ	800	٨٠٠	ض	ثَمَانِينَ	80	٨٠	ف	سَبْعَةً	7	٧	ز
تِسْعَمَائَةٍ	900	٩٠٠	ظ	تِسْعِينَ	90	٩٠	ص	ثَمَانِيَّةً	8	٨	حَ
أَلْفاً	1000	١٠٠٠	غ	مَائَة = مِئَةً	100	١٠٠	ق	تِسْعَةً	9	٩	ط
								عَشْرَةً	10	١٠	ى

Each letter of the Arabic alphabet has a numerical value (as above). It follows the order of the old Semetic alphabet and is used for numbering paragraphs, items, names and dates in history, etc.

أَبْجَدْ هَوَّزْ حُطي كَلَمنْ سَعفَصْ قُرِشَتْ ثَخِذْ ضَظِغْ

مُخْتَصَــرَاتٌ

Abbreviations

Meaning	Origin	Abbreviation
Mentioned after the name of the Prophet Mohammed, means: "May God bless him and save him	صَلّى اللّهُ عَلَيه وَسَلَّمَ صَلَّى اللّهُ عَلَيهِ وَسَلَّمَ	صَلْعَم ص
After the names of other prophets, means: "Peace be upon him."	عَلَيهِ السَّلامُ	عم
After the names of saints and prophet companions, means: "May God be pleased with him."	رَضِيَ اللّهُ عَنْهُ	رض
"There is no deity but Allah!"	لاَ إلَهَ إلاَّ اللّهُ	هَلَّلَ
"Allah is the greatest!"	اللّهُ أَكْبَرُ	كَبَّرَ
"There is no strength nor power but in Allah!"	لاَ حَوْلَ وَلا قُوة إلاَّ بِاللَّهِ	حَوْقَلَ
"God is enough for me and He is the best guardian."	حَسْبِيَ اللّهُ وَنِعْمَ الوَكِيلُ	حَسْبَلَ
The end/finished	اِنْتَهى	أهـ = هـ
"I bear witness that there is no God but Allah, and that Mohammed is the messenger of Allah."	أَشْهَدُ أَلاَّ إلَهَ إلاَّ اللّهُ وَأنَّ مُحَمَّداً رَسُولُ اللّهِ	تَشَهَّدَ
Etc./and so forth	إلَى آخِرِه	الخ

Meaning	Origin	Abbreviation
"There is no deity but Allah who is the One and has no associate."	لاَ إِلَهَ إِلاّ اللّهُ وَحْدَه لا شَرِيكَ لَهُ	وَحَّدَ
"Mercy of Allah be upon him!"	عَلَيْهِ رَحْمَةَ اللّهِ	تَرَحَّمَ
"I seek protection with Allah from the curse of Satan."	أَعُوذُ باللّهِ مِن الشَّيْطَانِ الرَّجِيم	عَذْبَلَ
"Come to prayers!"	حَيّ عَلَى الصَّلاة	حَيْعَلَ
"Come to prosperity!"	حَيّ عَلَى الفَلاح	

مُلْحَقٌ

Appendix

قَوَاعِدُ لُغَوِيَّةٌ

Grammar Notes

Conjunction (see footnote, p. 17) العَطْفُ

Conjunctions حُرُوفُ العَطْفِ are certain particles which unite two parts of speech, two nouns or two verbs. The second always takes the case of the first. Here are some common conjunctions:

Particle		Indication of Meaning
وَ (الواو)	and	Indicates mere combination with order
فَـ (الفَاء)	then	Indicates the second part comes immediately after the first
ثُمَّ	and then	Indicates the second part comes with delay after the first
أَوْ	or	Implying a sense of choice
أَمْ	or	Occurring in an interrogative sentence
لا	not	A negative particle
لٰكِنْ	but	Rectification
حَتَّى	even	Inclusion

Prepositions (see footnote, p. 25) حُرُوفُ الجَرِّ

A preposition حَرْفُ الجَرِّ is a word used with a noun or pronoun to show its relation to some other word in the sentence. After a preposition a noun takes the genetive case. Here are some common prepositions:

from	Indicates beginning	لِلابْتِدَاءِ	مِنْ
to	Indicates ending	للانْتِهَاءِ	إِلَى
on, over	Indicates superiority	لِلاسْتِعلاءِ	عَلَى
in	Indicates place or time	لِلظَّرْفِيَّةِ	في
as	Indicates similarity	لِلتَّشْبِيهِ	كـ (الكاف)
for	Indicates possession	لِلْمِلْكِيَّةِ	لِـ (اللام)

Pronouns (see footnote, p. 25) الضَّمَائِرُ

There are five different categories of pronouns in Arabic:

1. Personal Pronouns الضَّمَائِرُ
2. Demonstrative Pronouns أَسْمَاءُ الاشَارَةِ
3. Relative Pronouns اَسْمَاءُ اَلْمَوصُولِ
4. Interrogative Pronouns اَسْمَاءُ الاسْتِفهَامِ
5. Conditional Pronouns اَسْمَاءُ الشَّرْطِ

1. Personal pronouns الضَّمائرُ

Personal pronouns which assume the nominative case are set out below. They take the nominative case in the following situations:

a) as subject of a nominal sentence المُبْتَدَأ
b) as doer (subject) of a verb الفَاعِلُ
c) as substitute of a doer نَائِبُ الفَاعِلِ

ضَمائرُ الرَّفِ المُنْفَصِلَة

A. Detached Pronouns (Nominative)

Translation	Example	Pronoun		Person
I am a teacher	أَنَا مُدَرِّسٌ	I	أَنَا	1st (speaking)
We are teachers	نَحْنُ مُدَرِّسُونَ	We	نَحْنُ	
You are a teacher	أَنْتَ مُدَرِّسٌ	You (m)	أَنْتَ	2nd (addressed)
You are a teacher	أَنْتِ مُدَرِّسَةٌ	You (f)	أَنْتِ	
You two are teachers	أَنْتُمَا مُدَرِّسَانِ	You (m.d.)	أَنْتُمَا	*
You two are teachers	أَنْتُمَا مُدَرِّسَتَانِ	You (f.d.)	أَنْتُمَا	
You are teachers	أَنْتُمْ مُدَرِّسُونَ	You (m.pl)	أَنْتُمْ	
You are teachers	أَنْتُنَّ مُدَرِّسَاتٌ	You (f.pl)	أَنْتُنَّ	
He is a teacher	هُوَ مُدَرِّسٌ	He	هُوَ	3rd (absent)
She is a teacher	هِيَ مُدَرِّسَةٌ	She	هِيَ	
They are teachers	هُمَا مُدَرِّسَانِ	They (m.d.)	هُمَا	
They are teachers	هُمَا مُدَرِّسَتَانِ	They (f.d.)	هُمَا	
They are teachers	هُمْ مُدَرِّسُونَ	They (m.pl)	هُمْ	
They are teachers	هُنَّ مُدَرِّسَاتٌ	They (f.pl)	هُنَّ	

*For further explanation on the singular dual and plural, see p. 112.

ضَمائِرُ الرَّفْعِ المُتَّصِلَة

B. Attached Pronouns (Nominative)

Translation	Example	Pronoun	Person
I studied	دَرَسْتُ	I تُ	1st (speaking)
We studied	دَرَسْنَا	We نَا	
You studied	دَرَسْتَ	You (m) تَ	2nd (addressed)
You studied	دَرَسْتِ	You (f) تِ	
You two studied	دَرَسْتُمَا	You (m.d.) تُمَا	
You two studied	دَرَسْتُمَا	You (m.d.) تُمَا	
You studied	دَرَسْتُمْ	You (m.pl) تُمْ	
You studied	دَرَسْتُنَّ	You (f.pl) تُنَّ	
He studied	دَرَسَ (هُوَ)	He * (هُوَ)	3rd (absent)
She studied	دَرَسَتْ (هِيَ)	She ** (هِيَ) تْ	
They studied (2 boys)	دَرَسَا	They (m.d.) ـا	
They studied (2 girls)	دَرَسَتَا	They (m.d.) تا	
They studied	دَرَسُوا	They (m.pl) وُا	
They studied	دَرَسْنَ	They (f.pl) نَ	

*Words in parentheses mean implied pronouns.
**This تْ is not a pronoun but a sign of feminine gender.

The accusative personal pronoun is always the object of the verb and personal pronouns which assume the accusative case are set out below:

ضَمَائِرُ النَّصبِ المُتَّصِلَةِ وَالمُنْفَصِلَة

Attached and Detached Pronouns (Accusative)

Attached		Detached	Person
Equivalent	Pronouns		
He praised me	مَدَحَنِي	These pronouns no longer have common usage	1st
He praised us	مَدَحَنَا		(speaking)
He praised you (boy)	مَدَحَكَ		
He praised you (girl)	مَدَحَكَ		2nd
He praised them (m.& f.d.)	مَدَحَكُمَا		
He praised them (men)	مَدَحَكُمْ		(addressed)
He praised them (women)	مَدَحَكُنَّ		
He praised him	مَدَحَهُ		
He praised her	مَدَحَهَا		3rd
He praised them (m.& f.d.)	مَدَحَهُمَا		
He praised them (men)	مَدَحَهُمْ		(absent)
He praised them (women)	مَدَحَهُنَّ		

Genetive pronouns are always suffixed to a noun or preposition; they function as the second part in a constructed phrase or as object of a preposition:

ضمَائرُ الجَـرِّ

Attached and Detached Pronouns (Genetive)

Attached		Detached	
Equivalent	Pronoun	Equivalent	Pronoun
With me	مَعِي	My son	وَلَدِي
with us	مَعَنَا	our son	وَلَدُنَا
with you (boy)	مَعَكَ	your son (boy)	وَلَدُكَ
with you (girl)	مَعَكِ	your son (girl)	وَلَدُكِ
with you (m.& f.d.)	مَعَكُمَا	your son (m.& f.d.)	وَلَدُكُمَا
with you (men)	مَعَكُمْ	your son (men)	وَلَدُكُمْ
with you (women)	مَعَكُنَّ	your son (women)	وَلَدُكُنَّ
with him	مَعَهُ	his son	وَلَدُهُ
with her	مَعَهَا	her son	وَلَدُهَا
with them (m/f.d)	مَعَهُمَا	their son (m/f.d)	وَلَدُهُمَا
with them (men)	مَعَهُمْ	their son (men)	وَلَدُهُمْ
with them (women)	مَعَهُنَّ	their son (women)	وَلَدُهُنَّ

2. Demonstrative Pronouns أَسْمَاءُ الاشَارَةِ

Number	Masculine	Feminine
Singular	This is a boy هَذَا وَلَدٌ	This is a girl هَذِهِ
Dual (nominative)	These are 2 boys هَذَانِ	These are 2 girls هَاتَانِ
Dual (accus. & gen.)	These are 2 boys وَلَدَانِ	These are 2 girls هَاتَيْنِ
Plural	Those هؤلاءِ هَذَيْنِ	Those هؤلاءِ

The initial هـ has long vowel (fatha) but is written irrrgularly without the alif. Sometimes an accent is put above it pointing at the omitted alif, thus: هَذَا

3. Relative Pronouns أَسْمَاءُ المَوْصُولِ

Number	Masculine	Feminine
Singular	Who اَلَّذِي	Who اَلَّتِي
Dual (nominative)	Who (2) اللَّذَانِ	Who (2) اللَّتَانِ
Dual (accus. & gen.)	Who (2) اللَّذَيْنِ	Who (2) اللَّتَيْنِ
Plural	Who اَلَّذِينَ	Who اللَّاتِي = اللَّائِي

اَسْمَاءُ الشَّرْط 4. Conditional Pronouns		اَسْمَاء الاسْتِفْهَام 5. Interrogative Pronouns	
He who	مَنْ	Who?	مَنْ ؟
Whatever	مَا مَهْمَا	What?	مَا ؟
		Why?	لِمَ ؟
When	مَتَى أيَّانَ	Where?	أَيْنَ ؟
		When?	مَتَى
Where	أَيْنَ	How?	كَيْفَ ؟
Wherever	أنَّى حَيْثُمَا	How much?	كَمْ ؟
		Which?	أيّ ؟
However	كَيْفَمَا	Particles introducing interrogative sentences	* هَلْ ؟ أَ ؟
Which	أيّ		

*These two particles introduce interrogative sentences and enquire about the condition of the verb, so the answer will be either yes نَعَمْ or no لا , i.e. either happened or did not happen, e.g. هَلْ جَلَسَ عُمَرٌ؟ نَعَمْ (جَلَسَ) لا (مَا جَلَسَ)

Questions employing all the other interrogative pronouns require a specific answer to the information sought, e.g.

Who is she? مَنْ هِيَ ؟ She is Hind - هِيَ هِنْدٌ

The Verb | الفِعْلُ (المُجَرَّدْ والمَزِيدُ)
(for further explanation, see p. 46)

The verb in Arabic denotes an action and its time (tense), so the grammarians consider it the heart of the sentence. This concept reflects the outlook of the Arabic mentality which always combined the abstract and the concrete, spirit and flesh and blood, Divinity and existence, faith and action, the inward and the outward of things, and so on.

As the verb is the root from which all other derivations, verbal or nominal, are formulated, the Arabs gave great attention to moulding it into specific, accurate and basic patterns.

The verb has two types:

a) - the divested verb (اَلْمُجَرَّدُ) is a simple verb which consists of three or four indispensible roots (radicals), e.g.

to roll دَحْرَجَ   to write كَتَبَ

- the trilateral (three letter) verb has six patterns and covers the majority of the verbs.

- the quadrilateral (four letter) verb has one pattern and covers the minority of the verbs.

All together there are (6 + 1) = 7 patterns of verbs.

Among the potential characteristics of the Arabic language is the possibility of creating and moulding from its derivation new words taken from the divested verb (الفِعْلُ المُجَرَّدُ), by which I mean the increased verbs (الأَفْعَالُ المَزِيدَةَ):

b) the increased verb (المَزِيدُ) is a derived form created or moulded by adding one, two or three of the so-called letters of increase, before or between the radicals, e.g.

انْفَتَحَ	فَاتِحٌ	فَتَحَ
to be opened	conqueror	to open, conquer
تَدَحْرَجَ	افْتَتَحَ	
to be rolled	to introduce, inaugurate	

There are ten letters of increase which are as follows:

س – ء – ل – ت – م – و – ن – ى – هـ – ا –

which, all together, make up the phrase - سَأَلْتُمُونِيهَا

The grammarians expressed the various word patterns by the basic root, to do -

فَعَلَ ;

the first radical is represented by فـ (الفَاءُ)

The second radical is represented by ـعـ (العَيْن)

the third radical is represented by ل (اللام)

Each of these three radicals is given the vowel of its equivalent in the measured word, thus:

(كَتَبَ = فَعَلَ) (فَهِمَ = فَعِلَ) شَرُفَ = فَعُلَ) الخ

For the quadrilateral (four letter) divested verb the basic root (فَعَلَ) is suffixed by lam لام, thus: دَحْرَجَ = فَعْلَلَ

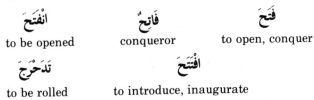

To measure an increased verb, add to the basic root the letter of increase, as they are; thus:

كَتَبَ = فَعَلَ   انْكَتَبَ = انْفَعَلَ   اسْتَكْتَبَ = اسْتَفْعَلَ

If a radical is omitted from the basic root, its equivalent in the measure is also omitted, e.g.

وَعَدَ = فَعَلَ   قَامَ = فَعَلَ

يَعِدُ = يَعِلُ   قُمْ = قُلْ

Adjectives (see footnote, p. 67)   النَّعْتُ = (الصِّفَةُ)

The adjective agrees with the qualified noun in cases of declension, gender, number, definiteness and indefiniteness.

الحالَة Case	المَنْعُوت Qual. noun	النَّعْتُ Adjective	Sentence الجُمْلَةُ
Nom.	تِلْمِيذٌ	مُجْتَهِدٌ	Omar is a diligent pupil عُمَرُ تِلْمِيذٌ مُجْتَهِدٌ
Nom.	الوَلَدَانِ	العَاقِلانِ	The two wise boys came جَاءَ الوَلَدَانِ العَاقِلانِ
Acc.	الوَلَدَيْنِ	العَاقِلَيْنِ	I praised the two wise boys مَدَحْتُ الوَلَدَيْنِ العَاقِلَيْنِ
Acc.	تُفَاحَةً	لَذِيذَةً	He ate a delicious apple اَكَلَ تُفَّاحَةً لَذِيذَةً
Gen.	حَدِيقَةٍ	جَمِيلَةٍ	I walk in a nice garden اَسِيرُ فِي حَدِيقَةٍ جَمِيلَةٍ
Gen.	القَمَرِ	المُنِيرِ	I look at the illuminating moon اَنْظُرُ الى القَمَرِ المُنِيرِ

Singular, Dual and Plural Nouns المُفْرَدُ والمُثَنَّى والْجَمْعُ

(see footnote, p. 103)

1. The singular المُفْرَدُ is the noun which denotes singularity, either masculine or feminine.

2. The dual المُثَنَّى is the noun which denotes duality, either masculine or feminine and it is formulated by adding:

   انِ to the singular in the nominative case, or

   يْنِ to the singular in the accusative and genetive case.

Dual		Singular		Case
Feminine	Masculine	Feminine	Masculine	
بِنْتَانِ	وَلَدَانِ	girl بِنْتٌ	boy وَلَدٌ	Nominative
بِنْتَيْنِ	وَلَدَيْنِ	girl بِنْتاً	boy وَلَداً	Accusative
بِنْتَيْنِ	وَلَدَيْنِ	girl بِنْتٍ	boy وَلَدٍ	Genetive

3. The plural الجَمْعُ is the noun which indicates three or more. It has three categories:

   a) Sound plural (m) جَمْعُ مُذَكَّرٍ سَالِماً which is formulated by adding the suffix

      ونَ to the singular in the nominative case, or

      ينَ to the singular in the acc. and gen. cases

   without changing the form of the singular, e.g.

Sound Plural Masc.		Dual	Singular		Case
players	لاَعِبُونَ	لاَعِبَانِ	player	لاعِبٌ	Nominative
players	لاَعِبِيْنَ	لاَعِبَيْنِ	player	لاَعِبًا	Accusative
players	لاَعِبِينَ	لاَعِبَيْنِ	player	لاَعِبٍ	Genetive

b) Sound plural (f. جَمْعٌ مُؤنَّثٍ سَالِماً which is formulated by adding the suffix:

اتٌ in the nominative case, or

اتٍ in the accusative and genetive cases without

changing the form of the singular, e.g.

Sound Plural Fem.		Dual	Singular		Case
*players	لاعِبَاتٌ*	لاعِبَتَانِ	player	لاعِبَةٌ	Nominative
players	لاعِبَاتِ	لاعِبَتَيْنِ	player	لاعِبَةً	Accusative
players	لاعِبَاتِ	لاعِبَتَيْنِ	player	لاعِبَةٍ	Genetive

c) Broken plural (m. and f.) جَمْعُ تَكْسِيرٍ which is formulated irregularly in various patterns by changing the form of the singular, e.g.

*Note the omission of the closed ة in the plural, and its change into ت in the dual.

Broken Plural		Dual		Singular		Case
Fem.	Masc.	Fem.	Masc.	Fem.	Masc.	
مُدُنٌ	اَوْلادٌ	مَدِينَتَانِ	وَلَدانِ	city مَدِينَةٌ	boy وَلَدٌ	Nom.
مُدُناً	اَوْلاداً	مَدِينَتَيْنِ		مَدِينَةً	وَلَداً	Acc.
مُدُنٍ	اَوْلادٍ	مَدِينَتَيْنِ		مَدِينَةٍ	وَلَدٍ	Gen.

وَالْحَمْدُ لِلَّهِ رَبِّ الْعَالَمِينَ

أ . هـ .

END